effective child protection

effective child protection

EILEEN MUNRO

SAGE Publications
London • Thousand Oaks • New Delhi

First published 2002

SAGE Publications Ltd
6 Bonhill Street
London EC2A 4PU

SAGE Publications Inc
2455 Teller Road
Thousand Oaks, California 91320

SAGE Publications India Pvt Ltd
32, M-Block Market
Greater Kailash – I
New Delhi 110 048

British Library Cataloguing in Publication data

A catalogue record for this book is available from the British Library

ISBN 0 7619 7081 9
ISBN 0 7619 7082 7 (pbk)

Library of Congress Control Number: 2002 102287

Typeset by C&M Digitals (P) Ltd., Chennai, India
Printed in Great Britain by The Athenaeum Press, Gateshead

ACKNOWLEDGEMENTS

I'd like to thank all of those students whose work has helped to develop my thinking and, in particular, those whose cases I have used. The students are Ramona Bridgman, Mary Brimson, Emily Campbell, Diana Miles-Ihle and Ann Sambidge. Thanks also to the Policy Studies Institute for giving me permission to reproduce Ann Hagall's *Perpetrator based risk indicators for dangerousness* findings which appear here as Table 5.1.

All of the cases have been radically altered so that any resemblance to real persons is purely coincidental.

For my daughters, Penny, Kate and Alice

contents

List of Illustrations

TABLES

FIGURES

1

introduction

Child protection work inevitably involves uncertainty, ambiguity and fallibility. The knowledge base is limited, predictions about the child's future welfare are imperfect, and there is no definitive way of balancing the conflicting rights of parents and children. The public rightly expect high standards from child protection workers in safeguarding children but achieving them is proving problematic.

Many initiatives to improve professionals' accuracy entail increasingly specific procedures, guidelines and risk assessment schedules. Front-line workers have mixed views about these, with many feeling that they undervalue the interpersonal skills of empathy and intuition needed to relate to parents and children. The issue is usually presented as a stark dichotomy between objective and subjective knowledge, science and art, or formal reasoning and intuition. This leads to a sterile and often bitter conflict. This book proposes that they are more usefully seen as on a continuum, with both being necessary, to some degree, at different stages in child protection work. I shall argue that the trained, experienced professional cannot be replaced with a bureaucrat with a set of forms, but he or she can be trained to use a broader, more reliable range of knowledge and to reason in a way that is more public and open to evaluation.

All advanced industrial countries have developed some type of child protection system. These societies recognise a child's right to a minimum level of care, protected from the worst excesses of parental abuse or neglect. At the same time, the privacy of the family and the rights of the individual adult are also highly valued, so that child protection workers have to walk a tightrope, balancing the conflicting rights of the family members. Moreover, the aim is not just to *minimise* the danger to children but to *maximise* their welfare. Removal from the birth family may increase their safety but harm their overall development. In all but the most extreme cases, the birth family is seen as the best place for a child to be nurtured. This affects the way allegations of abuse are dealt with. Professionals know that the parents they are investigating today are likely to be their partners in future efforts to improve family functioning. The way the initial contact is handled has long-term effects on the family's relationships with professionals.

In assessing a child's safety, accuracy is a crucial goal. Ideally, professionals want to be able to correctly classify parents as abusive or not, with the minimum of distress to those wrongly accused. They then want to manage the risk to children in a way that maximises their safety while also promoting their healthy development. Reality falls far short of this because of their limited knowledge. Added to this, they face strong pressures from the wider society. The image of a vulnerable child suffering pain and fear at the hands of their carers stirs up deep feelings of horror and outrage. Equally, the idea of powerful officials invading the privacy of the family and interrogating us on the intensely personal issue of our competence as parents provokes anger and resistance.

It is hard to imagine circumstances that pose a greater challenge to reasoning skills: limited knowledge, high emotions, time pressures, and conflicting values. It is not surprising, therefore, that so much effort and money have been poured into research to improve professionals' knowledge and skills. However, there is a problem in how many child protection services are trying to improve practice; the dominant view has been that progress can be achieved by a more formalised and prescriptive approach. The increase in empirical research and the development of guidelines, checklists, procedures and risk assessment instruments exemplify this approach. The problem is that many of the people who are on the receiving end of these developments – the front-line workers – are very sceptical about them and use them half-heartedly. There is a widespread feeling that they fail to capture key elements of working effectively with families. These formal aids are often seen as a device for protecting management from outside criticism rather than for protecting children from abuse.

This conflict of opinion in child protection reflects the classic debate about how to understand human nature. Should the social sciences study people with the methods used in the natural sciences, trying to describe an objective reality and developing causal explanations of behaviour? Alternatively, do the human skills of intuition and empathy offer a distinctive, and richer, form of understanding, enabling us to *know how it feels* to be another person? In relation to human reasoning skills, these contrasting views of knowledge are illustrated in the analytic/intuitive divide. At one extreme, analytic reasoning is formal, explicit, and logical. It is associated with mathematics and rigorous thought, where every step in the argument is spelled out. In contrast, intuition is inarticulate, swiftly reaching a conclusion on the basis of largely unconscious processes. In child protection work, analytic reasoning is exemplified by an actuarial risk assessment instrument where, on the basis of a set of questions, the practitioner works out a score that determines the level of risk to a child. Intuition, on the other hand, is illustrated by the practitioner who spends time talking to a family, drawing on professional experience to try and make sense of the family dynamics and develop a picture of how the family functions. The former is an intellectual task leading to a precise, impersonal conclusion. Its justification comes from the empirical work on which the instrument was based. The latter engages feelings and imagination as much as knowledge and leads to a conclusion that has an authenticity based on the individual's emotional response; it 'feels right'.

When we look at these extreme examples, we can see why front-line workers so often feel estranged from the formal developments in practice. The problem is not helped by the fact that the debate is often presented as a stark dichotomy. It frequently becomes heated and bitter, with the advocates of each side insulting the character of their opponents, who are either woolly brained (and so incapable of analytic thought) or emotionally stunted (and so unable to relate empathetically to others). There is, as a leading American academic has put it, a widespread belief that 'reason and caring are incompatible' (Gambrill, 1990: 360).

However, this is not the only, or the most useful, way of looking at the problem. Hammond (1996) has argued persuasively that it is more realistic to view human reasoning skills as on a *continuum*, with the purely formal, analytic methods at one end and blind intuition at the other. In between, intuitive reasoning can be more or less steered by explicit ideas or structured guidelines, and analytic methods may rely, to varying degrees, on intuitive skills in collecting and organising the necessary information. This picture of human abilities more closely resembles the experience of child protection workers who draw on all their reasoning skills in the total process of working with an abusive family, using both heart and head as required. It also provides a more accurate representation of the formal methods that are being introduced, few of which can be used without some intuitive skills. Instead of arguing that one type of reasoning is inherently superior to the other, conceptualising them as a continuum makes it possible to consider what degree of each is possible or desirable at a particular stage in the child protection process. This is, in essence, the project of this book.

The schism in the academic debate on reasoning skills has produced two distinct sets of literature. On one side, analytic theorists set out *prescriptions* for good reasoning, drawing on formal logic, probability theory and decision theory. The opposing school study how people actually reason and set out *descriptions* of successful and unsuccessful reasoning styles. The two approaches produce startlingly contrasting images of human thinking. The analytic thinker would approach a family in a cool and distant manner, using some formal instrument derived from empirical research to measure a specific dimension of family functioning and then would apply some statistical equations to compute the measure. The intuitive thinker will approach the task by establishing a rapport with the family, using empathy and experience to imagine how the family is functioning, and make some, largely unconscious, appraisal of their competence. It is easy to think of scenarios where each type could be inappropriate. In a family interview, where the father is getting increasingly aggressive, the intuitive thinker who makes a swift assessment of the

FIGURE 1.1 **The prescriptive model of decision making**

growing anger and its probable consequences would be much likelier to escape unharmed. The analytic thinker, stopping to get an anger rating schedule from his or her briefcase, is likely to exacerbate the situation. But in court, the positions are reversed. A child protection worker who asks that parents permanently lose custody of their children on the basis of a 'gut feeling' would be castigated by a judge, while a worker who can produce a detailed account of the reasoning behind the application is more likely to achieve the desired court order.

With decision making, the pictures from research are equally divergent. The *prescribed* image of a decision maker, looking at a range of options and weighing up their relative merits, is like Figure 1.1. However, people making decisions in everyday life are closer to Figure 1.2, navigating their way through a rough sea, making a sequence of small decisions 'to maintain a meandering course toward the ultimate goal' (Hogarth, 1981). The latter image perhaps more accurately conveys the process of conducting an investigation (with a procedure manual as a map) while the former seems a good model for making the major decisions about children's welfare, such as where they should live.

This book examines how child protection workers can become more analytic and critical in aspects of their work. I shall argue that they need to do so to improve their accuracy and make their reasoning more open and accountable. Formal methods, however, do not offer certainty and, with a subject like child abuse, we should be cautious about the level of

FIGURE 1.2 **The descriptive model of decision making**

accuracy we can realistically expect to achieve. This means that efforts to improve practice should not neglect or be dismissive of intuition. The centrality of intuition and empathy in practice needs to be acknowledged, and more formal methods seen as a way of building on, not replacing, these skills.

This book is concerned with the process rather than the specific content of practice. It does not, therefore, provide a comprehensive account of current policies or empirical research. Reference will be made, where appropriate, to this literature, but the central concern is to discuss how to use that material, to examine the reasoning processes involved in making judgements and decisions.

My own professional background is as a social worker in England and this affects the range of practice experience I can draw on. However, the topic of reasoning skills crosses national boundaries and so this book has international relevance. The subject also crosses professional boundaries: all the professions involved in child protection work have an active debate about relevant knowledge and skills, although the balance of support for the different positions varies. The book is, therefore, addressed to child protection workers, rather than social workers specifically.

OUTLINE

The next chapter examines the analytic/intuitive debate in more depth. It looks at how it has featured, historically, in the arguments about professional expertise and training and how it is currently revealed in the divergent strands of child protection practice and research.

Child abuse is a phenomenon shaped by its social context. It is quite unlike a specific disease entity, such as measles, where it can be hoped an understanding of its cause and treatment that has universal application can be developed. A society's views on child protection are a reflection of its views on children and families generally. Parents' ability to cope is strongly influenced by the degree of social support given to families. Chapter 3 looks at the range of cultural attitudes to families and the varying balance that countries draw between individual autonomy and social solidarity. These views have repercussions on attitudes to abusive parents and whether the emphasis is on rescuing children or supporting those parents to improve their standard of care.

The social dependence of the concept of child abuse has pervasive implications. Chapter 4 examines the problems of defining abuse and the consequences these problems have for research (and amassing a body of empirical knowledge), for policy (and formulating it in a way that can be consistently understood and implemented), and for practice (and the difficulties of getting agreement between the various people involved in a case).

The next two chapters look at the issue of assessing the risk of child abuse. Chapter 5 concentrates on the theoretical issues, explaining the role of probability theory in formal approaches and risk research, summarising current findings on risk factors, and examining the relative strengths and weaknesses of actuarial and clinical approaches to risk assessment. Chapter 6 deals with the practical processes, setting out a framework and then going through it in detail, exploring the difficulties that arise at each stage and discussing what types of reasoning skills are needed to resolve them.

Chapter 7, by far the longest in the book, addresses the question of how to manage the identified risk. It sets out the two main approaches in decision making research: the descriptive approach that has studied how people actually make decisions, and the prescriptive approach that draws on probability theory and decision theory to construct a model of rational decision making. The former body of literature offers useful insights for decision making under pressure of time. However, the major decisions in child protection work need to be made in a way that can be explicitly explained and justified to others and, for these, decision theory provides a good framework for organising and guiding one's reasoning.

None of the aids to assessing or managing risk hold out the promise of infallibility or remove the role of the professional thinker. There is, however, a large body of research on the reasoning errors people tend to make and this is a fruitful source of ideas about how mistakes can be detected and minimised. Chapter 8 starts by looking at the social context in which the reasoning is done and how this can help or hinder good reasoning skills, before examining how individuals can develop a more critical and open-minded approach to practice.

The final chapter summarises the key points in the book and discusses the implications for implementation: how can training promote both formal and intuitive reasoning skill; how can practice aids be developed that are integrated with intuitive skills; and, perhaps most importantly, how can agencies develop a culture that encourages critical thinking.

Throughout the book, I use case studies as examples. Some of these come from published accounts of practice (e.g. in public inquiry reports into child deaths) but most come from the students who have taken the child protection course I teach at the London School of Economics. I would like to reiterate the point made in the Acknowledgements that, for the sake of confidentiality, not only have these cases been rendered unrecognisable, but also any distinctive features have been altered, so if readers find a resemblance to a case they know, this is a chance coincidence.

SUMMARY

- Child protection workers have to make complex judgements and difficult decisions in conditions of limited knowledge, time pressures, high emotions, and conflicting values.
- Analytic and intuitive reasoning skills are best seen as a continuum, not a dichotomy.
- The centrality of empathy and intuition needs to be acknowledged, but practice can be improved by developing professionals' analytic skills.

2

expertise in child protection work

Today's arguments about the relative importance of analytic and intuitive knowledge have a long history in the caring professions. It is useful to look at this history because it reveals how polarised the arguments between art and science used to be. This old rigidity has been eliminated as developments in philosophy have modified the positions of both sides (Chalmers, 1983; Munro, 1998). Although misguided, however, this dichotomy is still influential, leading people to take an extreme view of their opponents' arguments and underestimate the degree of shared ground. These outdated assumptions need to be challenged so that analytic and intuitive thinking can be seen as on a continuum rather than as extreme opposites.

This chapter begins with a detailed case study to illustrate the range of knowledge and skills typically used in child protection work. I then use the history of social work training as an example of how the changing arguments about knowledge have influenced professional training and practice. In the current debates, the analytic tradition is apparent in the strong movement towards evidence-based practice, the introduction of formal instruments for assessing risk and making decisions, and the increasing proceduralisation and formalisation of practice. I shall examine the strengths and weaknesses of these developments, and argue that there is still a crucial and central place for intuitive knowledge within child protection work.

A Case Example

The following extracts from a student's account of how she dealt with a referral give some idea of the complexity and variety of reasoning skills involved, as she moved from an initial referral for a step-parent adoption to an assessment that the children were at high risk of abuse.

A couple, Doris (aged 44) and Ron (aged 49), had married two years previously and were now applying for a step-parent adoption of Doris's two daughters by a previous marriage, Mary (aged 10) and Pamela (aged 6). The social worker, who was experienced in this type of referral, first made some background checks that revealed no adverse information and then made a home visit:

Even before I entered their home, it was apparent that orderliness was important to the family. The porch, windows and high perimeter fence were so new that the latter was still dripping with preservative. It occurred to me that these barriers might be to keep the world out as much as the family in. When I was only allowed to enter the home once I removed my shoes, and the adults talked proudly about the substantial refurbishments they had undertaken, it seemed that cleanliness was vitally important too.

Ron was neat and tidy, wearing a cardigan and slippers, a slim, mild mannered, grey haired man with a cultured speaking voice. He seemed eclipsed by the size and forcefulness of his wife – an articulate, middle-aged lady of heavy build. She was opinionated and forthright, talking of her dissatisfaction with 'The Authorities' and her pride in complaining. To reinforce this, she said she had transferred her children to another school when discipline was too lax; she changed her doctor when he would not prescribe medication she demanded. Although not directly stated, I received a clear warning about having to conform to Doris' expectations.

The couple then went on to speak vehemently about the need to discipline children and then told the social worker of the problems they were having with the younger daughter, Pamela, who was vomiting and soiling herself frequently, eating like an animal, and displaying behavioural problems at school.

Throughout, Doris talked aggressively and negatively about Pamela, describing her as 'a beast, a hateful child, a horrible little brat'.

The child was heard arguing with her sister and was summoned into the room by her mother:

She had a rather waxen, pale complexion and dark shadows under her eyes and she cowered, hanging her head whilst her mother proceeded to criticise, harangue and shame her.

The way the couple spoke of, and to, the girl was so unusual in a stepparent adoption case that the social worker felt very suspicious and, after completing the initial interview, proceeded to make a thorough investigation of the family's history and functioning. In doing this, she faced strong resistance from the mother:

When asked, Doris was overtly hostile about providing details of family history and the references that are legally required for an adoption application. Conversations with her were like being drawn into a verbal maze, leading to dead ends where she looked blandly at me and asked 'how can you expect me to remember after all this time?' I was very careful not to enter into a confrontation with her, recognising that she was trying to set up a battle with me but eventually Doris responded to my request and produced amended police reference forms.

With this basic factual information to guide her search, the social worker was able to make contact with several professionals who had had contact with the mother: social workers, teachers, general practitioners, adult and child psychiatrists, and police officers. She pieced together that the mother had a history of drug abuse and depression and had been diagnosed as having a 'psychopathic personality disorder'. Also, two adult children had been removed permanently from her care in childhood because of physical and emotional abuse. Pamela's schoolteachers were very concerned about her, regarding her as an unhappy, friendless little girl with behavioural and learning difficulties.

With this range of information, the social worker began to consider that Pamela might be the victim of emotional abuse but, first, discussed the difficulty of diagnosing emotional abuse:

> Authors generally agree that there is no one definition of emotional abuse. Gabarino et al. (1986) suggest that particular patterns of behaviour used by parents or primary caregivers cause emotional abuse and include rejecting or isolating behaviour, terrorising the child, ignoring him or her, corrupting or mis-socialising the child. Iwaniec (1995) offers the definition: emotional abuse can be overtly rejecting behaviour of carers or passive neglect. Carers who persistently criticise, shame, rebuke, threaten, ridicule, humiliate, put down, induce fear and anxiety, who are never satisfied with the child's behaviour and performance (and do so deliberately to hurt the child) are emotionally abusive and cruel. Equally those who knowingly distance themselves from the child by ignoring signals of distress, pleas for help, attention, comfort, reassurance, encouragement and acceptance are emotionally abusive and neglectful. Research by Benoit et al. (1989) shows that 96 per cent of emotionally abused children have interactional problems with their mothers. Iwaniec's own study (1983) suggested that children subject to emotional abuse have serious attachment problems.

Pamela's early years had been problematic. She had been conceived after her mother's first marriage had ended. The father deserted Doris in the early stages of the pregnancy. Doris said she had never bonded with her daughter.

> In considering the prerequisites for healthy psychological development, Bowlby (1984) states the need for secure attachment. Similarly, Erikson et al. (1989) reiterate that unless a child receives appropriate love and positive encouragement from infancy onwards it is impossible to make the necessary psychological progress from one developmental stage to another, which ultimately results in a 'whole' personality. Both Skuse (in Meadows, 1997) and Adcock (1995) suggest that a repeated cumulative pattern of persistent verbal abuse in a low warmth/high criticism environment is more damaging than an isolated, injurious incident. I was beginning to form a picture of Pamela living in such circumstances.

The mother's history of conflict with professionals suggested that she would not work in partnership with the local authority. It was feared that a precipitous move into a formal child abuse investigation might antagonise her to the extent that she might refuse further contact, making it harder to collect sufficient evidence to warrant coercive intervention. The social worker therefore continued contact on the basis of pursuing the step-parent adoption, asking to interview the two girls without the parents present, as would be usual in such a case:

> Although Pamela had not been advised of my visit she readily engaged with me. Both girls were serious and earnest. We talked minimally about adoption – I deliberately played this down – and primarily about the children's day to day life. They confided that they get into trouble at home where punishments are severe. Both described how each, but Pamela especially, is excluded 'for weeks at a time' to her bedroom. They said they exasperated their mother and the adults responded by hitting them with a stick, leaving red weals on their palms. The girls agreed that Pamela got the worst of it, sometimes beaten on her bottom too. I was bothered that the children told a complete stranger about this so soon after meeting them, and wondered aloud what they thought might happen if the adults knew of this conversation. The girls were uncertain but were explicit that they wanted me to know although they did not expect me to do anything about it.
>
> I weighed up how I might deal with this situation. Would confronting the adults result in a greater risk of physical abuse to the children after I had left the home? I decided it could do so, so instead queried the level of 'chastisement' that the adults use, without being more specific. They said the worst punishment they use, after withholding of privileges, is sending the girls to their bedrooms.

The social worker concludes that the children are experiencing a significant level of physical and emotional abuse. She weighs up the risk of this abuse continuing or escalating, using Greenland's (1987) and Browne and Saqi's (1988: 68) lists of risk factors, and judges that the mother, Doris, poses a very high risk as an abuser. She also notes the history of this family and how similar the current picture is to twenty years ago when Doris's eldest son was removed from her because of abuse. Her decision that the case needs to be dealt with as a child protection investigation means the end of her involvement, the case being transferred to a child protection team, who will have to decide whether to try and preserve the family. Is there any therapeutic option that can be offered with a significant chance of success or should the decision be to repeat history and remove the girls?

The student concludes her case study by considering the parents' motivation. She is puzzled that they sought an adoption order and, so, exposed themselves to scrutiny, particularly in light of the mother's previous, hostile contact with Social Services in relation to her older children. She speculates that the diagnosis of 'psychopathic personality disorder' may be relevant:

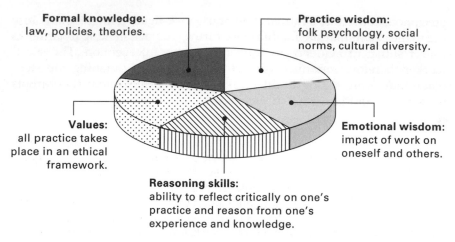

FIGURE 2.1   **Categories of knowledge and skills**

My understanding of psychopathic personalities is not only that they are antisocial but that true psychopathic personalities are unable to appreciate or anticipate the consequences of their actions. Consequently, I speculated that maybe Ron did not know all the history and that Doris had not realised the impact this history would have on the application. Alternatively, perhaps this couple are so exasperated with Pamela that they cannot tolerate living with her but to request her removal from their home would not sit easily with their religious beliefs. Is their hidden agenda for the local authority to remove her, ostensibly against their wishes?

THE NATURE OF EXPERTISE

The range of knowledge and skills that the student was using in this case can be classified into five major categories (Figure 2.1).

Formal knowledge   Training provides child protection workers with knowledge of the law, policies and procedures as well as covering a range of theoretical knowledge and research about child development, family dynamics and methods of intervention. In the previous example, the social worker is clearly working within a specific framework of law and procedures that shape her duties and powers. She is also using formal theories of child development and adult mental disorder. Empirical research evidence is cited on the impact of particular forms of parenting behaviour on children. She uses research on risk factors to weigh up the level of danger for the children.

Practice wisdom   Everyone develops skills in making sense of their own and other people's behaviour. The student demonstrates use of this everyday 'folk psychology' in her interviewing skills. She also demonstrates a specialist understanding gained through her previous experience with step-parent adoptions that gave her a background against which to find this referral very unusual. Her skills in interviewing children about abuse are a combination of an ordinary ability to talk to children enriched by her training and practice in raising such sensitive and painful issues.

Her final comment on the case, where she is trying to make sense of the parents' decision to seek a step-parent adoption, reveals one of the main features of our everyday way of explaining behaviour; we assume that people are rational. By this we do not mean that they always act in the most sensible way but that their actions are intentional and can be explained by reference to their beliefs, feelings, and wishes.

In this case, the social worker is puzzled. In general, one might expect that if a mother was wanting to keep a reconstituted family together, she might well consider a step-parent adoption as a means of strengthening the stepfather's commitment to the family and, therefore, it is rational for her to apply for one. However, Doris had good reasons from past experience to believe that if the family was scrutinised by professionals, as inevitably happens in the course of an adoption application, then there was a high probability that they would be concerned about the children's welfare, as all previous professionals had been. So, far from strengthening the unity of the family, the process of seeking an adoption was likely to lead to its break-up. To make sense of this otherwise perplexing action, the social worker speculates that Doris did have a realistic idea of the probable consequences of her action and, in fact, covertly wanted that outcome.

In reasoning this way, the social worker was assuming some kind of rationality principle. Although there is considerable philosophical debate about the precise wording of such a principle, one simple version is:

> Given any person, X, if X wants D and X believes that A is a means to attain D, under the circumstances, then X does A. (Rosenberg, 1988: 25)

Emotional wisdom Child protection work stirs up feelings in families and workers. The social worker demonstrated an ability to understand and deal with the emotional impact that the work had on herself and others, using it as a source of understanding of both the family's and her own behaviour. She experienced the mother as a threatening, aggressive woman and the younger girl's sad demeanour aroused her compassion and concern. She was also aware of the dynamics of interviews with the mother and felt she was being tugged into a head-on, destructive conflict where the mother could conform to her pattern of clashing with professionals. She took deliberate steps to avoid an open dispute that would provide the mother with a means of breaking off contact with her.

Values All aspects of work need to be seen within an ethical framework, including awareness of discrimination in all its forms. This case presented the classic issue of how to balance the rights and needs of both parents and children. Removing a child from the birth parent(s) is a rare and extreme step to take because of the values society attaches to parenthood. Children, however, have a right to be protected from harmful abuse and neglect and, in this case, the professional dilemma was whether their rights could be met while also respecting the parents' rights. If the two are incompatible, the British legal system currently states quite explicitly that the child's welfare is paramount but this view has varied over time and between societies.

Reasoning skills If we consider how the social worker was reasoning in terms of the analytic/intuitive continuum, we can see that she moved along the continuum at different stages of the investigation. Intuition and empathy are most apparent in her direct contact with the family.

She was very aware of her 'gut reaction' to the family, of feeling that the parents were very concerned with cleanliness and discipline and that neither parent showed affection or compassion for the younger girl. But her interactions with the family were not simply intuitive and unreflective. While talking to them, she was also thinking about what to do, drawing on explicit lessons drawn from her training or work experience. When she thought about the family outside the interviews, she was using formal theories and research to guide her reasoning. She drew on theories from psychology to assess the quality of the parent-child relationship. She used an assessment framework derived from research to assess the risk of abuse. The decision on what to do involved a conscious appraisal of both the risks and benefits to the children if she referred the case to the child protection team.

This account of practice illustrates the use of both analytic and intuitive knowledge, and of explicit and implicit reasoning. In this, research suggests that she is fairly typical, although, if anything, she is more able than average to formulate her use of theory and the steps in her reasoning (Secker, 1993; Walker et al., 1995; Marsh and Triseliotis, 1996).

UNDERSTANDING HUMAN ACTIONS: THE ANALYTIC/INTUITIVE DEBATE

Few would deny that all of the five elements above play a part in practice, but debates have flourished on their relative importance. Reflecting debates in the social sciences in general, the caring professions have always debated how best to understand their clients, patients, or users and there have been conflicting views on what type of skill and knowledge base they can, or should, lay claim to. One option is to draw on the methods of the natural sciences and try to develop causal explanations of why people behave as they do. In this model, the formal knowledge component of practice is the most important and, as theory and research develop, will become increasingly the basis for action, making practice wisdom redundant. Contrary to this is the view that human beings are significantly different from objects in the natural world and, as fellow human beings, we have the special talents of empathy and intuition for understanding them. This type of understanding is encapsulated in our folk psychology and practitioners' practice wisdom.

In medicine, the search for formal knowledge has been dominant but this approach has been criticised for underestimating the importance of the doctor/patient relationship and the influence this has on the patient's recovery or deterioration. Clinical psychologists, too, have favoured the natural science route in research and training, but practitioners tend to place more value on intuition and empathy, leading to a split between academia and front-line work (Sobell, 1996).

If we take as an example the history of social work in Britain (which has always been strongly influenced by American social work), we can trace the impact of the debate about knowledge.

People have been helping each other since human societies were formed. Informal support from family and friends has always been provided. In the past, formal support tended to be offered mainly by religious groups. Beyond the sixteenth century, Britain had a minimal level of state provision under the Elizabethan Poor Law. The development of more systematic forms of help began in the nineteenth century, as in other developed countries, as industrialisation and urbanisation removed people from their informal support networks.

The charity workers of the nineteenth century began the debate about what type of knowledge and skills they should rely on. The caseworkers of the Charity Organisation Society (COS) in Britain and the USA, the precursors of present-day social workers, relied on common sense and practical knowledge to make their assessments. The crucial issue was to distinguish between the deserving and undeserving poor. Would applicants for aid be able to make constructive use of it or would a grant be harmful, reinforcing their laziness and depravity (COS, 1890)? When they offered help to a deserving applicant, they did not just offer material aid but a supportive relationship to guide and encourage the needy in tackling their problems. Mary Richmond, the author of the foremost American textbook for caseworkers, asserted the importance of: 'the tonic influence which an understanding spirit always exerts' (Richmond, 1917: 200).

In developing a helping relationship, caseworkers relied on their everyday skills rather than any formal body of knowledge. However, the nineteenth century also saw the burgeoning of the social sciences, offering new theories for understanding individual and social actions. Opinions differed on whether the social sciences should or could use the methods of the natural sciences in studying people or whether they should continue to rely on empathy and intuition in speculating about what was going on in other people's minds (for a fuller account, see Munro, 1998).

Critics of the scientific approach tend to stress that its supporters were anxious to acquire some of the kudos of the natural sciences. A similar line of argument in social work is that the scientific school are trying to put social work on a professional basis and so attain a higher social status. The advocates of a scientific approach respond by pointing to the reason for the high status of the natural sciences: their success in developing well-corroborated theories that can be productively used to manipulate events in the world. The technological advances of the nineteenth century provided, for many, convincing evidence of the value of this method of studying the world.

In turning to the social sciences for guidance, the first set of theories adopted were from sociology and economics, theories that drew attention to the external constraints on individuals' behaviour. Caseworkers had assumed that the individual had to change to function better in society but social research highlighted the powerful effects of social and economic factors on individuals' choices. The economic recession at the end of the nineteenth century created high unemployment, making it clear that the unemployed were not just work-shy. Empirical studies of poverty by Booth (1889) and Rowntree (1902) identified the main causes of poverty as being a lack of jobs, low wages, illness and old age – factors not readily under the individual's control.

Social theories offered ideas on how to intervene at a policy level to improve people's lives and fuelled influential movements for social and political change. To front-line workers, however, they seemed to provide little practical advice on how to deal with the families on their caseloads. Psychology proved to be the more valuable source. In the 1920s, interest in psychological theories flourished, offering, as they did, direct guidance on how to help people. Psychology, however, offered two contrasting models of scientific theory. On the one hand, strict behaviourists modelled themselves explicitly on the natural sciences, and concluded that they should focus on the study of observable behaviour and avoid the difficulties of studying mental processes that were not directly perceptible. On the other hand, psychoanalysis looked specifically at what was going on in people's minds, speculated about its causation, and offered therapeutic methods for helping them. It fitted much more harmoniously with the existing common-sense approach to practice and proved to be far more attractive to social workers than behaviourism. Although both schools of psychology have continued to enjoy support, psychoanalytic theories dominated training in Britain and the USA for many decades.

Freud claimed that his theory was scientific, but this has long been disputed (Farrell, 1981; Grunbaum, 1985; Eysenck, 1986). Indeed, the eminent philosopher Karl Popper's interest in studying the philosophy of science was triggered by his experience as a social worker in Alfred Adler's child guidance clinics in Vienna, where he was struck by his colleagues' ability to make any evidence fit their psychoanalytic explanations of someone's behaviour (Popper, 1963). This apparent immunity to falsification led him to explore the nature of science and how it differed from other forms of theorising, such as psychoanalysis.

Irrespective of its scientific status, psychoanalysis's claims to effectiveness as a form of therapy have been seriously challenged by evaluative studies. Both psychoanalytic therapy and its modified use by social workers have failed to demonstrate that they have an appreciable impact on analysands or clients. In the 1950s and '60s, American social workers, confident of the value of their methods, conducted many, large-scale, controlled trials on practice. They were shocked by the results:

> Lack of effectiveness appears to be the rule rather than the exception across several categories of clients, problems, situations, and types of casework. (Fischer, 1973: 19)

Losing confidence in psychoanalysis, social workers looked for alternative theories to guide their work. Some adopted behavioural approaches, impressed by their demonstrated effectiveness on specific problems. But many, still deterred by its mechanistic view of humanity, looked elsewhere and, in the 1970s, the curricula of training courses expanded rapidly to include numerous new theories, e.g. social systems theory, crisis intervention, task-centred casework, communication models, and humanist and existentialist models. These theories ranged across the art/science divide, making comparison between them problematic since they embodied different methodologies and epistemologies. Students faced the daunting task of choosing between them. An American academic sympathetically described their position:

> Consider the plight of the typical recent graduate of a social work program whose head is cluttered with this diversity of constructs and theories. Where does one begin in the attempt merely to assess the client? Should the focus be on the client's ego strengths, social role, psychosocial patterns, personality traits, or status in his or her system? Or, should the focus be on the family's interactions, communication patterns, selected external re-enforcements, or what? (Goldstein, 1986: 354)

The range of theories presented problems to the student not just in how to choose between such a diverse set but also in how to use them. Courses covering so many rival approaches were unable to give much time to any individual one and so students tended to acquire a very sketchy understanding that led to an imprecise use, if any, in practice. In Britain, research on the outcomes of social work training indicated major shortcomings in graduates' ability to apply any theoretical approach explicitly and competently (Walker et al., 1995; Marsh and Triseliotis, 1996).

At the same time as theories proliferated, the reliability of scientific methods came under attack. Logical positivism, the orthodoxy in the 1920s, was shown to have irreparable defects. In its place, empiricists offered a modified philosophy that made lesser claims to truth but still held that information gained through our senses provided evidence against which a theory could be tested and that theories that withstood rigorous testing were more reliable than untested ones (Newton-Smith, 1981; Kuhn, 1978). But some have seen the death of logical positivism as also the end of any claims of science to produce more reliable knowledge than other methods of study. Relativists have argued that there are no objective criteria for theory appraisal and that science is like every other discipline in having its own internal rules that have no external or universal standing. Therefore, social workers were encouraged to be sceptical of the advocates of science and to choose for themselves which theories they thought made sense as the basis for their practice. One academic described the process of theory choice as intimating that the individual student 'pays her money and takes her choice' (Howe, 1987: 166).

The reason for going into these historical details is not to revisit the major philosophical debates about methodology in both the natural and social sciences (for a detailed discussion, see Munro, 1998) but to illustrate the backdrop against which today's drive for more explicit, critical, evidence-based practice is operating. Critics of an analytic approach often attack an extreme, and now obsolete picture, disregarding or unaware of the major changes in its assumptions. They present science as still operating within a positivist framework, making unsustainable claims to objectivity and reliability, and denying the importance of values or of studying the mind in theorising about behaviour. Unfortunately, some advocates provide ammunition for these attacks by making exaggerated claims for evidence-based practice or risk assessment schedules, and dismissing intuitive skills as trivial. Therefore, I want to offer a more balanced account of the relative contributions of formal and intuitive knowledge to practice.

The detailed example of practice I quoted at the beginning of this chapter illustrates the application of both sources of knowledge at different stages of the process of working directly with a family. The question is of what balance can and should be achieved. While academic debates are generally presented in a very polarised way, practitioners tend to avoid extreme positions. Most have continued to rely heavily on their intuitive and empathic skills, enriched by some knowledge of theories and therapies, and, in child protection, increasingly guided by procedures and checklists whose use is dictated by management.

One point of view is that intuitive knowledge is inferior and should be gradually replaced by formal knowledge as empirical research increases the scientific store of knowledge. This, I think, is seriously wrong. Intuition plays an irreplaceable part in reasoning about people and a consideration of its strengths will help to show that the practitioners who resist academic calls to become wholly scientific have some rational grounds for valuing their intuitive skills. Psychological research shows that both analytic and intuitive processes are involved in making judgements and decisions (Hastie, 2001: 662). The intuitive processes seem to be fundamental, providing a swift response, often with emotional content. The analytic processes seem to be optional and involve a more deliberate, conscious consideration of the issue. Hammond (1996) proposes a cognitive continuum framework, where pure intuition and pure analysis anchor a descriptive scale in which most of our reasoning is some mixture of the two ingredients.

THE STRENGTHS OF INTUITIVE REASONING

The key strength of intuition is speed; it enables people to draw a conclusion from a vast range of variables almost instantly. Its swiftness makes it essential in the intense atmosphere of direct work with families. Interpersonal skills have to be deployed intuitively. This is not to say formal research and knowledge have no part to play. Research on the core components of counselling – empathy, unconditional positive regard and genuineness – provides details of what behaviours convey these qualities most effectively and students can be trained to express them more clearly. However, when actually interviewing a family, the worker needs to be fluent enough to respond instantly; for the most part, it is not feasible to hesitate and consult a manual before deciding how to answer a question.

Intuition also has the advantage of drawing on people's background knowledge of human behaviour and society that has been built up over a lifetime. This is so wide-ranging and complex that it is, in practical terms, impossible to spell out completely. It was once an ambition of behavioural psychologists to reduce all terms referring to mental states to descriptions of behaviour and context (Carnap, 1975). This seemed feasible because of the way people learn to use psychological terms. A child learns when it is appropriate to use words such as anger or sadness to describe someone's mood from hearing people use them in particular settings and learning to correlate their use with specific facial expressions and circumstances. Since language is public, there must be some observable features that help people learn the rules of use. Critics have demolished the reducibility thesis by showing that it is, in practice, impossible to carry out because of the *complexity* of the background knowledge that informs the use of language (Scriven in Krimmerman, 1975; Putnam, 1978). In practice, too, behaviourists have not pursued this approach (Zurriff, 1990). It is indeed quite hard to talk about human behaviour without including reference to the thought processes behind it; to say that Peter is talking to John is to do more than describe behaviour – it also tells us something about his intention in speaking.

The essential role of intuitive background knowledge is most eloquently described by Polanyi, who coined the phrase 'tacit knowledge' to describe it and argued that it also plays an inescapable role in the natural as well as the social sciences (Polanyi, 1967). Saying that background knowledge cannot be fully articulated does not mean that it is some mysterious, intangible entity that cannot be examined. It may not be possible to write out a formal account of every stage of reasoning but some progress can be made in saying how a particular judgement or decision was reached. In an interview, a practitioner may intuitively decide that the mother is becoming increasingly hostile and respond accordingly. If the worker is asked later for the grounds for this judgement, it will be possible to identify aspects of the woman's body language, the content of her speech and the tone of her voice that the worker was drawing on in making the inference. It is unlikely, however, that any practitioner could specify all the rules that would define all of the above signs, and only the occasions when the judgement of hostility would be made.

A final point in defence of intuitive skills is to emphasise their usefulness. They have been, and continue to be, the backbone of people's ways of making sense of the world and each other, and, in many situations, clearly work well enough. Historically, the vast majority of people would have been unable even to read and write and, therefore, unable to use the more formal, analytic methods, yet they survived.

THE LIMITATIONS OF INTUITIVE REASONING

Intuition has limitations, however, and it is these weaknesses that have led to the continuing search for more analytic ways of developing knowledge.

First, intuitive knowledge is mainly implicit and only partially articulated. Hence, it is defective as a source of public, shared knowledge. In social work, for example, experienced practitioners develop practice wisdom. This may be shared with others in direct contact, through case discussion or supervision, but the wisdom dies with the worker. It does not lend itself to the gradual compilation of a professional, public body of knowledge that can be taught to other students.

A second limitation is that it generates only low-level theories or generalisations with a small range of application. In contrast, scientific methods encourage the creation of abstract theories that attempt not only to describe regularities in the world but also to explain them in terms of underlying processes. An intuitive knowledge of grieving, based on observing or experiencing it, allows people to identify the range of feelings and behaviours that tend to cluster under the term and to have some idea of the path the process of grieving takes. In contrast, a formal theoretical explanation of grief, such as that proposed by Murray Parkes (1986), offers a deeper explanation of what underlies the observed feelings and behaviour. It can be used to make predictions about how long it may last and under what circumstances we might expect someone to need professional help in moving on. It also supplies therapeutic principles for those wishing to help the grief-stricken.

The third major problem with intuitive knowledge is its reliability. People obviously learn from experience, realising that some of their intuitive conjectures are misguided and discarding them. It is also possible, as I shall discuss in Chapter 8, to be more critical in examining one's intuition. There are, however, some constraints on rigorous testing that are only resolved by using formal research methods. The main argument for evidence-based practice is that its findings have been more rigorously evaluated than our intuitive knowledge and therefore should be considered more reliable. The key problems that research methods try to solve are the range of our experience and the biases in our perceptions. It is not my intention to give a detailed account of research methods (since this would be too lengthy) but only an overview of the main principles that illustrate why formal research improves on individual appraisal. There are numerous texts on the subject for those wanting more comprehensive information (e.g. Atherton and Klemmack, 1982; Burns, 2000).

Sample Size and Representativeness

Psychology research shows that people are always looking for generalisations and regularities in the world, ways of reducing the vast, bewildering array of experiences to a more manageable, comprehensible state. Enthusiasm tends to make people rush to judgement prematurely. Someone only needs to see a few instances of drug addicts accompanied by grubby, unkempt children to start believing that drug addicts do not take good care of their children's physical needs. This generalisation might well be wrong because it is based on a small, possibly unrepresentative, sample. The type of drug the addicts take may be significant in affecting their standard of child care. It may be a correlate of drug addiction, such as poverty, that produces the finding, so that there is no direct causal link between drug addiction and the children's appearance. The setting in which the drug addicts were seen may contain a biased range of addicts. A clinic in an inner-city location may have a different clientele than one in an affluent rural area.

Researchers try to overcome such problems by studying a large sample and selecting it in a way that aims to minimise bias so that the people studied can be assumed to be representative of the wider group.

Biased Observation

People have an overwhelming tendency to notice any evidence that can be construed as supporting their beliefs and a blind spot when it comes to evidence that contradicts them (Baron, 1994). One particularly unpleasant consequence of this is that it contributes to the maintenance of prejudices and racism. Those who believe black men are violent will notice any case of a black man involved in a violent incident, and see it as confirming their prejudice, but can meet countless non-violent black men without pausing to wonder whether the belief in their violence is false.

In child protection, this tendency manifests itself when, for example, a worker who thinks a family is making progress makes a home visit. All the signs of progress will readily come to the worker's attention but contrary evidence is not so easily collected. It takes a conscious effort of will (or use of a checklist) to counter this bias. (The issue is dealt with in greater detail in Chapter 8.)

In clinical work generally, it is a common finding that people who have put great effort into helping an individual or family have an understandable hope that their efforts have been useful and, so, are biased in their observation of progress.

Rival Explanations

A child protection worker who has been working with an abusive family for six months may see many signs of progress on factors that had caused concern. The physical standard of child care may have improved; the parent/ child relationship may appear more warm and loving. At first glance, it might seem reasonable for the worker to argue: 'I have tried to change variables X and Y. X and Y have changed. Therefore I caused the change.'

But evaluating the effectiveness of professional help presents many problems because of the complexity of the influences on human behaviour. There are several rival explanations that might be true and need to be ruled out before the worker can take the credit for the improvement:

- The family might have been receiving help from other sources and these were more influential. Perhaps the mother had psychiatric treatment for depression and the improvement in her mood led to the observed gains in her level of parenting. The extended family may have been as concerned as the child protection service about what was happening and become more supportive. The worker's efforts are only one of the many influences acting on a family's behaviour at any time.
- The change might be due just to the natural process of maturing that everyone experiences (to varying degrees). Many of the families referred to child protection services have very young parents who will tend to develop more of the necessary qualities for parenting as they get older, whether or not professional help is given. It is known from psychological research that people are not static but change and grow over time.
- The worker's observations of improvement may be the result of wishful thinking. Having tried so hard to help the family, you have a tendency to see what you want to see. Inquiries into child abuse deaths continually describe how workers who had rehabilitated an abused child in the birth family persist in believing the child is doing well despite evidence that should cause concern. Stephanie Fox, for instance, suffered forty incidents of bruising over a year (including four black eyes), yet the child protection conference were able to write

to the parents that the professionals saw no cause for concern about their parenting (Wandsworth Area Child Protection Committee, 1990).

- The improvement may be due to the parents realising what evidence the professionals want to see (or what behaviours they want to see discarded) and providing this without there being any fundamental change in their attitude to their children. Therefore, it may be wrong to assume that change on these variables proves the parents have truly changed.

- Finally, even if the workers are right in thinking they have caused or contributed to the change in any one family, it cannot be assumed that the method of helping would work with all other families. If the worker has repeated success with a number of families, it becomes more plausible to believe it has wider application, but the cases any one worker deals with are but a small part and probably drawn from a narrow geographical or social range, so that more research is needed to identify which families it does work with.

All of these alternative explanations for progress have to be considered against the worker's claim to have helped the family. Formal research methods are designed to test them. The power of a particular research design can be defined as the number of rival, plausible explanations that it rules out (Campbell and Stanley, 1966). A single case study is weak because it leaves unanswered questions about the natural history of the problem – what would have happened without professional intervention? A controlled trial is stronger because it directly examines whether the treated group show greater progress than a similar group of people who are untreated.

THE STRENGTHS OF ANALYTIC REASONING

Analytic developments can be applied to both the content and the structure of reasoning in child protection work.

In relation to content, empirical research seeks to develop the knowledge base for child protection work. All aspects of the subject have been studied to some degree: how common is abuse; who is likely to be abusive; what are the causes and the long-term effects on the child; what factors improve professionals' ability to predict future harm; which methods of intervention are effective and with whom? There has always been some tradition of research in child welfare but, in recent years, the drive to encourage practitioners to use empirical evidence has increased markedly. Articles and books on 'evidence-based practice' have proliferated (see Table 2.1). One factor behind this is that social changes have reduced the power and autonomy of professionals, who are now subject to far higher demands for public accountability and so need to justify

TABLE 2.1   **References on evidence-based practice**

Gough R. (1993) *Child Abuse Interventions*. Edinburgh, HMSO.

Kluger M., Alexander G. and Curtis P. (eds.) (2001) *What Works in Child Welfare*. Washington, DC: Child Welfare League of America.

Macdonald G. (2001) *Effective Interventions for Child Abuse and Neglect*. Chichester: Wiley.

Web pages on practice-related research findings:

www.cochraneconsumer.com

www.elsc.org.uk

www.ex.ac.uk/cebss

their decisions and actions. Another factor is that enough research has been conducted to provide a useful body of findings to guide practitioners.

Evidence-based practice comes at a price. Practitioners cannot just rely on what they have learned in their basic training but need an on-going commitment to keeping up-to-date with research. For this reason, a number of efforts have been made to provide resumes and critiques of research.

In addition, although the argument for empirical research rests heavily on the greater reliability of its findings, the scientific approach highlights the speculative nature of all knowledge. Scientific theories are never proven absolutely; at best, they are only more and more strongly corroborated by the evidence; at worst, they are falsified and have to be discarded. The approach, therefore, encourages all professionals to be willing to question their existing assumptions about families and possibly reject them if the evidence is strongly against them. It requires the child protection worker to tolerate the insecurity of knowing he or she is acting on imperfect knowledge.

THE LIMITATIONS OF ANALYTIC REASONING

For the professional with a heavy caseload of families who need help *now*, one problem with our current knowledge base is how limited it is. Findings are tentative and, at best, show a correlation or weak causal link between factors. Poverty is associated with a higher rate of child abuse but it is still true to say that the majority of poor parents are not abusive. Many studies on the effectiveness of different interventions with abusive families are of a weak design, not allowing us to rule out alternative explanations for perceived signs of progress and to assert confidently that the professional help was decisive. Professionals cannot just read the findings of research. They also need some understanding of the issues around research design in order to read studies critically and appraise the reliability of the results. For this reason, many of the resumes of research findings include comments on the methodological strengths and weaknesses of the studies.

Currently, many of the formal aids to judgement and decision making that are available have not been empirically tested. This is particularly true of risk assessment schedules that have been developed by different teams and are increasingly being adopted by agencies. Even where a schedule has been tested on its local population and shown to be more reliable than clinical judgement, it needs to be retested if exported to a different cultural context.

Another problem is that much of the research is not conducted in one's own country. For British child protection workers, the greatest source of empirical findings is the USA where there is a stronger research tradition and considerably more money to fund research. This gives workers the difficult problem of deciding whether the results can be generalised to their own country. North American studies have found that stepfathers are more likely to be abusive than birth fathers (Daly and Wilson, 1985) and this finding is frequently used in risk assessment schedules. However, similar research in Sweden has found stepfathers were no more likely than birth fathers to be abusive (Temrin et al., 2000). One explanation for these conflicting findings could be the differences between Swedish and North American societies, clear evidence of the cultural dependence of research. This leaves professionals in other countries to wonder which society most resembles their own. An alternative explanation is that the Swedish data are much more recent and reflect are social changes in Western countries in relation to re-formed families that alter the level of danger stepfathers pose to their stepchildren. This would suggest that the North American results were now out-of-date and inaccurate.

This one topic illustrates how evidence-based practice offers no simple prescriptions for practitioners. Empirical evidence requires judgements about its reliability and its applicability in the worker's own context.

Some of the limitations of research will be reduced as more studies are conducted but some are more enduring. One problem lies in the nature of the core concept of child abuse itself. As I discuss in Chapter 4, the concept of abuse is socially constructed, varying between societies and over time. It is unrealistic to expect to develop universal, enduring theories about a subject whose meaning is ambiguous and changing.

Another set of problems arise from the difficulties, both ethical and technical, of conducting rigorous research on such a personal area as family interactions. If researchers are testing the effectiveness of a particular treatment model, they can rarely use the classical clinical design of a controlled trial where families are randomly assigned to the treatment or to a control group who receive no treatment. This design allows us to tell whether people improve whether or not they receive any treatment. In child abuse, however, once we know that a group of children are suffering abuse, it is not ethically acceptable to assign them to a non-treatment group just for the sake of research. They can, at best, be assigned to a group being offered an alternative type of treatment, leaving open the question of what happens to untreated families.

Another problem lies in the sheer expense of doing the necessary research. Current theories about the causation of abuse see it as the result of numerous interacting factors, such as social context, relationships within the family, and the individual psychology of the family members. It is hard to tease out the contribution of one particular factor in such a complex model unless very large samples are used. Such studies are very expensive to conduct and, consequently, are rare.

As all its proponents would agree, empirical evidence, at most, provides one essential component in decision making. Case management as a whole, however, requires the professional to consider many other factors as well. Ethical considerations limit what can be done. Removing a child is, evidently, a very effective way of protection from harmful birth parents but its use as a solution is limited by the value we ascribe to the rights of parents to care for their own children. Economics also places constraints on decisions. The cost of removing children is often, in practice, more important than ethics in deterring professionals from taking this action. The cost of various treatment options can be as important in weighing up a decision as the evidence on their effectiveness.

Finally, formal theories provide only one aspect of the knowledge and skills needed by a front-line worker. Intuitive and empathic skills are essential in relating to a family, eliciting their co-operation to the extent that it is possible to collect the information needed to use theories and formal aids to reasoning. As I have been arguing, the practitioner has to move along the analytic/intuitive continuum at different stages in the process of working with a family. The old-style debate where formal knowledge and intuition are seen as rivals battling it out for supremacy is sterile. We need to see them as complementary and focus on how they can be integrated.

The work of Dreyfus and Dreyfus (1986) offers an interesting twist to this picture of a continuum. They studied what happened to doctors as they became more expert at making a diagnosis. As learners, they operated at the analytic end of the spectrum, using checklists or a formal outline for gathering a history from a patient. As they became more experienced, they became more and more intuitive, absorbing this analytic model into their background thinking so that they did not have to draw on it in any conscious way. Doctors who then became teachers developed the ability to act intuitively but also to explicate their reasoning later to students to show them how they reached their diagnosis. That is, they became skilled as reflective practitioners.

These findings cannot be applied directly to child protection work. Medical students do not possess from the beginning an intuitive understanding of their subject. Asked to perform brain surgery, they do not have an amateur's working knowledge of how to do this. They need formal training to even begin to perform the task. Novices in child protection, in contrast, already have the vast array of folk psychology to use in making sense of individuals and families. Where medical students move from analytic to intuitive use of knowledge, child protection students require an extra step:

(folk) intuitive – analytic – (expert) intuitive

CONCLUSION

The issue of finding a way of integrating analytic and intuitive knowledge seems to me crucial to overcome the hostility so many practitioners feel towards efforts to make them more explicit and critical in their work. It needs to be recognised that there are significant differences between the two forms of knowledge in terms of how they are experienced by the worker. Empathic understanding provides a rich picture of what a person is experiencing. An explanation using a formal theory is an intellectual, not an emotional experience. Moving between one type of understanding and another therefore needs to be recognised as a difficult process. In the later chapters of this book, I attempt to offer ways of improving judgement and decision making that recognise and respect both forms of understanding.

SUMMARY

- Child protection work is intellectually and emotionally challenging, requiring the full range of human reasoning skills. Practitioners use formal knowledge, practice wisdom, emotional wisdom, and ethics in working with families.
- The old-style debate where formal knowledge and intuition are seen as rivals battling it out for supremacy is sterile and, in the light of developments in the philosophy of science, obsolete. We need to see them as complementary and focus on how they can be integrated.
- Efforts to improve practice by developing formal aids to reasoning need to recognise the essential role of intuitive skills and build on them, not dismiss them as insignificant or worthless.

3

the social context

INTRODUCTION

The 1989 United Nations Convention on the Rights of the Child, now ratified by all members of the UN except for Somalia and the USA, sets out the principles and standards for the treatment and care of children. Article 19 specifically addresses the issue of child abuse:

> State parties shall take all appropriate legislative, administrative, social and educational measures to protect the child from all forms of physical or mental violence, injury or abuse, neglect or negligent treatment, maltreatment or exploitation, including sexual abuse, while in the care of parent(s), legal guardian(s) or any other persons who have care of the child. (p. 318)

At first glance it might seem that there is a high level of international agreement on children's needs and rights; that child protection services could be expected to have a lot in common. However, the convention reflects a set of aspirations for children's well-being and social status that is not yet, in reality, achieved in any country. Indeed, for vast numbers of the world's children, it is remote from their reality of being exposed to war, famine, drought, flood, illness, or chronic poverty. Also, when we move from the high levels of abstraction found in the articles of the convention to the specific way each country perceives and treats children, we find considerable diversity. Societies vary in their basic concepts of childhood and family, in their beliefs about the relationships between children and parents, and in the relative duties and powers of parents and the state.

The protection of children from harm at the hands of their parents and carers occurs within a social context that shapes every stage of the process. On one level, the reasoning processes are international; the logical structure of making judgements and decisions is constant. However, the content of those judgements and decisions is a product of the society in which they are made, from the initial assumptions about what counts as abuse, to professionals' duty and power to intervene, the options available to them, and the relative desirability of different possible solutions. The current form of any child protection system is a product of its culture and history. It also needs to be understood in relation to the state's attitude to families and children more generally and the type of help states offer all parents, not just abusive ones, in caring for their children.

The importance of social factors is illustrated by Briggs and Cutright's (1994) study, where an international comparison of infant homicide rates in twenty-one countries between 1965 and 1988 was made. It was found that indicators of family stress, available resources, female status and a culture of violence all had significant independent effects on the rate of infant homicide. They also reported that the higher the percentage of women in the labour force was, the lower the percentage of women compared with men enrolled in tertiary education, and the higher the rape rate was, the higher the infant homicide rate.

This chapter covers a great deal: the development of today's concept of childhood, and of family policy in general and child welfare services in particular, the current tensions in the welfare state system, and changing social patterns and structures. It also ranges from an overview of industrialised countries to a focus on British history as an illustrative example. My aim is to demonstrate the importance of social context in child protection and to identify some significant social and economic changes that will have an unknown impact in the future.

PERCEPTIONS OF CHILDHOOD

The concept of childhood as we now know it in advanced industrialised countries is relatively recent. In the past, children predominantly were seen as having special needs only for the brief time that they were physically dependent on others for survival. Once they reached the age of five or six and were capable of basic self-care, they joined the adult world of work and play. In the sixteenth century, the age of legal adulthood in England was ten. Girls were often married off by that age, and boys a little later. For most there was no formal education. 'Life was rude and there was not much to learn' (Aries, 1962).

A new vision of childhood developed among the rich in the sixteenth and seventeenth centuries where it was seen as a period of innocence and play, free from the duties of adulthood. Aries suggests one practical reason for delaying adulthood was that armour had become too heavy for a child to wear and the sons of the elite could only be considered adult when they could fight alongside their fathers.

This special period did not apply to the majority of children, who were poor and expected to contribute to the family tasks as soon as they were physically capable. In farming communities, there was no sharp distinction between work and home or between private and public life. Nor were the boundaries of the family as well defined as in today's nuclear family so children's needs were met not just by the parents but by the wider community.

Debates about the nature of childhood and the needs of children have always reflected stark differences in the underlying perception of children's nature. They have been seen as both saints and sinners. The Romantic view, put forward, for instance, by Rousseau, is that children are saints; childhood is a time of innocence. They are born good but are gradually corrupted by the world. In childhood, therefore, they should be protected from the evils of the world, prolonging their state of purity for as long as possible. Evangelical religious views, however, such as those propounded by John Wesley, took the opposite position: children are born sinners and need to be disciplined into virtue. Parents were urged to 'break the will of your child' to 'bring his will into subjection to yours, then it may be afterward subject to the will of God' (Holloway, 1963).

The tragic case of James Bulger in England illustrates how both perceptions of childhood still persist in uneasy proximity. James, a two-year-old, was brutally killed by two ten-year-old boys. James captured the nation's sympathy as an archetype of vulnerable innocence. He was filmed on CCTV walking off trustingly with his killers. The perpetrators, meanwhile, were portrayed as the epitome of evil and depravity despite being so young themselves as to raise serious questions about their ability to understand fully what they had done. There was little interest in what experiences they themselves might have endured to lead them to such behaviour. Punishment rather than therapy or rehabilitation was the sentence most strongly desired by the public. This sentiment was still so strong, eight years later when they were released from prison, that they had to be given new identities, and there is a lifelong ban on the media revealing their new names or addresses, because of fears for their safety.

Whether saints or sinners, children are nowadays seen as only slowly acquiring adult capabilities and needing a long period of supervision and guidance before taking a full role in society. In developed countries, the place for that nurturing is typically seen as being the family:

> There is no generally accepted substitute for the family and its child production and socialization role, and there is increasing evidence that nurture and care in a context of love and individualization are essential to achieving the results that society values. (Zigler et al., 1996: 31)

The United Nations Convention on the Rights of the Child reflects the emerging concept of children in modern society as people with rights of their own, independent of the adults around them, and with complex needs to be met if they are to develop to their full potential. In this context, protection from abuse or neglect is only one of many requirements and societies have developed a range of other services for them and their parents, the quality of which helps or hinders their safety.

FAMILY POLICY

Public policies towards children and their families have now become an integral part of social policy in advanced, industrialised countries. I am using 'family policy' as the generic term for both the policies that are designed to affect the situation of families with children (e.g. maternal and child health policies) and those that have clear consequences for families (e.g. a taxation system that incidentally discourages a mother from part-time working). The premise underlying the formation of family policy is 'that society needs children, and needs them to be healthy, well-educated, and, eventually, productive workers, citizens, and parents' (Kamerman, 1996: 32).

British history provides a typical example of how state involvement in the lives of children and parents has increased. The Elizabethan Poor Law of 1601 made it the state's responsibility to step in if children were abandoned or destitute but it was of a very minimal and residual nature. If any relatives could be found, they were expected to take responsibility and any help provided took the form of getting the children work so that they could be self-sufficient.

From 1760 on, increasing urbanisation and industrialisation made the former support systems provided by the community and the church inadequate (Wilensky, 1975). People, hoping that work in industry would save them from the unending poverty of farming life, were beginning to move in large numbers from the rural communities into towns and cities.

Children's welfare was first to benefit from increased state regulation. For factory owners, children were a very useful workforce because they required less pay than adults and could get into small spaces in the machinery to operate or repair them. The horrors of factory work inspired reform. The motivation was a mixture of concern both for the child and for society. The risks to the child were of death, injury and stunted growth because of the poor diet and living conditions. Their moral development was also at risk because they were getting litte education or religious instruction. They therefore posed a danger to society as potential delinquents or criminals. Their earning capacity also threatened the authority of the father, who, as patriarch, was considered to have power over the rest of the family.

Initial interventions were of a very limited nature. The first factory act – the 1802 Health and Morals of Apprentices Act – restricted the working hours of pauper apprentices to twelve hours per day. Slowly and, for capitalists, very reluctantly, the state began to extend its range of social policies. As with the child labourers, the motivation was a mixture of self-interest and philanthropic concern for the quality of people's lives. The growth of working-class movements and revolution abroad raised the fear of rebellion if conditions were not improved. During the nineteenth and early twentieth centuries, legislation was introduced on public health measures, universal education, working conditions, and income maintenance.

At the end of World War II in 1945, social policies expanded radically. The war created an unprecedented level of social solidarity, leading to increased commitment to social justice and opportunity for all (Titmuss, 1958). The Beveridge Report (1942) set out an ambitious set of plans for tackling the five giants of ignorance, idleness, squalor, disease and want. It recommended a welfare state to provide services from the cradle to the grave, universal and free at the point of delivery.

Although some form of welfare state has emerged in all developed countries, there is considerable variation in the specific shape these states have taken. The incidence and nature of child abuse and neglect in any society are, in part, a product of the quality of other services available to parents in that society, and how easy or difficult a task it is for any parent to meet the demands of child rearing. Certainly, for the professionals trying to help abusive or neglectful families, the options available will vary radically.

Esping-Anderson (1990) has developed a widely accepted typology of ideal types of welfare regime in non-communist countries:

1. *Conservative corporatist*

   A highly occupational social insurance system where most benefits are related to employment. The principle of subsidiarity is important, encouraging the devolution of provision to the lowest possible level. It is said to reinforce existing class, gender and status differences and to discourage women from joining the labour force. Found in countries where the influence of the Catholic Church is strong – Austria, France, Germany and Italy.

2. *Liberal or neo-liberal*

   Mainly market-oriented, social insurance approaches to financial provision, with meagre, means-tested state benefits for the residual poor suffering from family or market failure. There tends to be a high level of stigmatisation because benefits are seen as disincentives to work. Social solidarity is not generally an important consideration. The 'Anglo-Saxon' model applies to the UK, the USA, New Zealand, Canada and Australia.

3. *Social democratic or Scandinavian*

   A universal insurance system and earnings-related benefits. It favours universal and equalising provision with a strong belief in social solidarity. It provides more family services than other regimes and is therefore said to give individuals, especially women, more freedom in the labour market. It is found in Scandinavian countries, including Iceland and Denmark.

While the major areas of welfare are health, education, housing and income maintenance, all of which have a significant impact on children's lives, all states also have a range of policies specifically aimed at helping families with their childcare responsibilities. There are three main elements to these policies: services, time, and financial support.

Health care and education are major services provided for children but the growing area is in childcare services for working parents outside the normal school hours. Countries vary greatly in how much help is offered and whether it is provided as a universal or selective service for vulnerable families. France, for instance, provides pre-school places for 97 per cent of children aged 3 to 6; compulsory schooling begins at 6. In the UK and the USA, state provision has been targeted at vulnerable families, mainly those known to the child protection services. The bulk of provision for ordinary families is by the private sector.

Time for parenting is the second element of provision. Maternity leave has existed in some form for more than a century although it is only since the 1970s that job protection has included protection from losing seniority and benefits. The length of childbirth-related leave varies from three months in the Netherlands to three years in Austria and Finland (Kamerman, 1996: 44). There is now increasing provision of parental (not specifically maternal) leave to cover family responsibilities in later childhood. In the European Union, the need for parental leave was recognised in 1989 in the Social Chapter; this should have formed part of the Maastricht Treaty but the idea was such anathema to the British government of the time that it had to be put into a separate document that Britain refused to sign. The Labour government subsequently accepted it.

Financial support typically includes some form of child benefit or family allowance, maternity allowances to replace income forgone as a result of childbirth, housing allowance, and additional benefits for parents on low incomes or special needs such as a child with disability. The level of financial support is extremely varied, leading to substantial differences in the rate of child poverty.

The following data are all from Bradbury and Jantti (2001). Relative child poverty rates in the OECD member states in the mid-1990s ranged from 3.4 per cent in Finland to 26.3 per cent in the USA. Even within the European Union, relative rates varied from 3.4 per cent in Finland to 21.3 per cent in the UK. The regional differences within the USA are as large as within the European Union, a matter of some significance since the USA has recently shifted most of its anti-poverty policy from the federal to the state level. The dominant world trend is one of increasing relative child poverty, with the most dramatic increases in Russia, Hungary, Italy and the UK. The Nordic countries figure strongly among those with decreases (or negligible increases) in child poverty, together with France, Canada, Spain, Israel and, most prominently, Taiwan.

A more detailed examination of the statistics in the UK found that certain groups are particularly likely to be in poverty (Piachaud and Sutherland, 2000: 5):

Families with four or more children	(73%)
Families with mothers aged 16–24	(68%)
Ethnic minority families	(65%)
Lone parent, never married	(79%)
Lone parent, divorced or separated	(66%)
Families without a working parent	(86%)

Poverty has been experienced not just by particular groups such as lone parents but by whole areas. The changing pattern of industrial production meant towns and cities lost their main source of employment. There are estates where employment is the exception, children have never known a working parent, crime and drug abuse rates are high and the quality of the housing and local schools is poor. Children brought up in such places have few of the opportunities available to the majority. The growing polarisation between the reasonably prosperous and the very poor has led to the development of the concept of 'social exclusion'. The term, although notoriously ambiguous, means something more than just poverty but tries to capture some of its less tangible effects in terms of being able to participate fully in society. Debates on this issue reflect the persistent, conflicting attitudes of compassion and fear, of altruism and self-interest towards people in need. For Charles Murray, an American commentator, fear is the dominant emotion: social exclusion is leading to the creation of an underclass that is outside the norms of society, and that poses a threat to society by its involvement in crime, particularly drugs, and failure to be self-supporting or to raise its children as law-abiding, hard-working citizens (Murray, 1990). Frank Field, on the other hand, is motivated by compassion, defining the socially excluded in terms of the obstacles they face in playing a full role in society (Field, 1989).

Although poor parents can take excellent care of their children, the constant fight to meet their basic needs greatly increases the stresses on them. It is therefore not surprising that poverty is a major, though not universal, feature of the families known to child protection services. Ninety per cent of the children in public care in Britain come from families who are dependent on Income Support (Local Government Association, 1997: 3). Research has shown that, for families on low incomes, life is an unremitting struggle to meet the basic needs for food, heat and adequate clothing as well as a lack of opportunity to take part in activities that the rest of society takes for granted (Kempson, 1996; Middleton et al., 1997).

CURRENT TENSIONS IN WELFARE PROVISION

For much of the developed world, the 1950s and 60s were a time of prolonged economic growth and social stability, coupling a strong commitment to developing welfare states, with the financial resources to do so. However, the continuation of welfare states in their original form has been questioned by a number of developments in recent years: the demographic changes in the population, the globalisation of the economy, economic insecurity and high unemployment, leading to increasing poverty and social exclusion.

All developed countries are seeing major demographic changes. Life expectancy is rising and the birth rate is dropping so that the ratio of young to old (and of workers to retired people) is being transformed. In England and Wales, the percentage of the population over 65 was 5 per cent in 1901 and 16 per cent by 2001. Family structures are also changing. The number of marriages has decreased over the past 20–30 years in all European countries and cohabitation has become more and more common. In the UK, the proportion of couples aged 16–29 cohabiting has almost doubled to 40 per cent since the 1980s; a third of babies are born out of wedlock. Divorce rates have risen with four out of ten marriages in the UK expected to end in divorce. Lone parents now head a quarter of all families, the number having trebled since 1971. As a result of these changes, the traditional family consisting of a breadwinner husband and a non-working wife caring for dependent children accounts for a mere 8 per cent of all households.

Changing work patterns are also having significant effects on child rearing. Women with children are entering the labour force in ever greater numbers, leading to demands for better childcare provision and family-friendly employment policies such as paid parental leave and favourable part-time working conditions.

Globalisation of the world economies is also posing a threat to welfare states. The period after World War II saw prolonged economic growth in the developed world that provided the prosperity to fund policies aimed at promoting social justice. All countries, to varying degrees, increased welfare spending and made efforts to redistribute wealth and improve opportunities for all. The optimism of this period was founded on a sense of financial stability and a belief that full employment was a feasible policy goal. These assumptions, however, were shattered by the oil crises of the early 1970s. Spiralling inflation, a slowing down of economic growth, and rising unemployment led to huge increases in public spending, affecting international competitiveness and triggering debates about the longer term viability of generous welfare systems (Rhodes, 1996: 306).

The end of the Cold War and the collapse of the communist Soviet Union has also been a major catalyst in the development of international economic and political relations (Deacon et al., 1997). Fukuyama (1992) famously pronounced the 'end of history' and the universal triumph of western liberalism and capitalism. Some argue that the globalisation of the world economy will undermine the power of nation states to formulate their own economic and social policies (Geyer et al., 1999). In particular, it is claimed that, in order to be competitive in a world economy, they will have to reduce taxation and, hence, social welfare costs. Countries which have supported generous systems of welfare that promote social justice will have to scale down their public spending to the level of competitors, such as the USA, who have only a residual form of welfare. Within the European Union, it has been argued that universal welfare benefits should be reduced, with increasing targeting of benefits for those in need (EU, 1993). The OECD has warned that the pressures to create an economy attractive to capital (low taxes, free markets) could 'lead to governments being unable to meet the legitimate demands of their citizens for public services (cited in *The Economist*, 29 January 2000: 3).

This seemingly inevitable downward convergence of welfare systems has, however, been challenged (Hirst and Thompson, 1999; Stiemerling, 2000). Critics cite the evidence that in Europe, although all countries are having to restructure at a general level, there is still considerable diversity in the detail of the policies they pursue (Bonoli et al., 2000: 44). Despite all experiencing the same pressures from the globalisation of the economy, the way they react is mediated by their cultural history and existing social policies and structures. Sweden is cited as an example of a country with an exceptionally well-resourced welfare state that, if the globalisation thesis is correct, should be under particular pressure to downsize. But an OECD survey found that 'Sweden is peculiar in having both a generous social safety net and strict job protection' yet it 'outperforms most other countries in terms of relative income levels for key target groups such as families with children and old-age pensioners' (OECD, 1999).

Some question whether the decline in welfare states is inevitable because of the benefits they offer to capitalism. Although, at first glance, it might seem that capital will always prefer countries with minimal taxation and labour regulation, this is counterbalanced by wanting to invest in a country with political stability and a well-educated and trained labour force (Navarro, 2000). Residual welfare policies and a marked disparity in wealth between the richest and poorest create the climate for social instability and conflict.

The impact of the changing world economy has, therefore, been variable. In Britain, however, it has certainly been associated with a reduction in welfare spending and increased targeting and stigmatisation of those in need of state help. The Conservative governments between 1979 and 1997, all sharing a neo-liberalist philosophy, oversaw a radical reorganisation of the welfare state, with strategies aimed at introducing market forces to improve efficiency. In a period that saw steep rises in unemployment, benefit levels were cut, with a shift from universal to selective provision. Welfare was seen as a burden on the economy that should be pared to a minimum, a marked change from the Beveridge philosophy of providing universal services to help the whole population from the cradle to the grave. But 'there is much debate about whether the changing British economic policy in the 1980s was a rational response to the 'globalization' trends ... or whether they reflected a distinct ideological and political attack on the old system of political economy' (Gough, 1998: 110).

The dominance of neo-liberal politics in many industrialised countries in the 1980s and '90s has led to many changes in welfare that have made the task for many parents and, consequently, for child protection professionals much harder. There are fewer universal services to support them and less public willingness to help, and the families referred to child protection services are likely to be poorer and experiencing increasing stigmatisation.

Neo-liberalism is, however, being challenged by new interpretations of socialist doctrines. Left-of-centre parties have been elected in many countries, parties attempting to put into practice 'third way' or 'modernised socialism' policies (Giddens, 2001). These parties have abandoned the traditional socialist ideas of economic management and planning but want to mitigate the irrationality and injustice of the free market economy. Giddens sketches the key differences between left and right politics:

> To be on the left is to want a society that is solidary and inclusive, such that no citizen is left outside. It is to have a commitment to equality and a belief that we have an obligation to protect and care for the more vulnerable members of society. As a crucial addition, it involves the belief that the intervention of government is necessary to pursue these objectives. Rightists are liable to deny each of these propositions. (2001: 5)

In Britain, New Labour came to power with a commitment to improving public services and reducing child poverty and social exclusion. Its success or failure will have major repercussions for family life and the quality of childhood. At the international level, the political fight continues with variable repercussions for child protection services.

THE DEVELOPMENT OF CHILD WELFARE AND CHILD PROTECTION SERVICES

Statutory services have three main areas of responsibility:

1. To provide alternative care for children who, for some reason, cannot be cared for by their birth families.
2. To support families and help them meet their children's needs (this includes parents whose children have special needs such as physical disability).
3. To investigate and protect children considered to be at risk of abuse or neglect from their carers.

Although, nowadays, all three elements are explicitly valued, their relative importance varies between countries, shaping different priorities in child protection agencies. As a rough generalisation, the English-speaking countries (Britain, the USA, Canada, Australia, and New Zealand) put most resources into the investigation and protection services while continental Europe places most emphasis on family support services (Hetherington et al., 1997; Pringle, 1998).

A look at British history illustrates how the basic framework of child welfare is a product of the wider society's views and how professionals' range of choices is restricted by these outside forces so that a child protection service is always tailored for a particular country.

Significant Developments in Child Welfare

The relative importance of each of the elements of services for children has varied greatly over the decades. The 1601 Poor Law dealt only with the first category of taking responsibility for orphans. Historically, the state has been very reluctant to intervene in the intimate relationships between family members whether to help or police them. The privacy of the family was seen as an essential power base in a liberal society.

The first formal intervention was only indirect, dealing with foster, not birth, families. The Infant Life Protection Act of 1872 reflected the growing social concern about baby farming, where large numbers of babies were fostered in one household to free the mothers for work. This Act required carers with more than one baby under one year old to register with the local authority and be subject to some inspection.

The quality of children's life came under more scrutiny as it became more public in the nineteenth century and, so, revealed the effects of poverty and deprivation. Their attendance at school showed teachers the extent of mental and physical handicap in the population, much of it the effects of poor diet and care. The Boer War at the end of the century also revealed the physical consequences of poverty: large numbers of working-class recruits were so weak they were no use to the army.

The motivation to respond to these signs of deprivation came partly from a fear that the race was degenerating and as a result Britain would become too weak to compete in a world economy and partly from direct concern for the welfare of the working class. It was helped by the growing group of middle-class women with the time and motivation to be philanthropic (Parton, 1985).

There was increasing psychological understanding of the causal importance of families in bringing up healthy and moral children. Neglect or excessive discipline could both be destructive, leading to death or serious problems in adulthood. This led to the start of the National Society for the Prevention of Cruelty to Children (NSPCC), based on the American example. This charity's pressure led to the 1889 Prevention of Cruelty to Children Act, which put a limit on how violent a father could be – but it still allowed considerable scope for chastisement. The NSPCC had a steady rise in referrals; by 1910 over 50,000 cases were being investigated annually. At this time, though, poverty, not parental cruelty, was the major killer. A third of children in poor areas did not reach their first birthday; it was such a common experience in their work that NSPCC officers were given lessons in hygiene about handling dead bodies. Of the cases they dealt with, 80–90 per cent were classed as neglect and only 7–10 per cent as ill-treatment. Child cruelty was seen as a class-based problem, restricted to the poor.

The NSPCC was also aware of child sexual abuse in the family (although it is often claimed that it only came to recognition in the 1980s). The number of identified cases, however, was small. In 1910, less than 1 per cent of their referrals were classed as criminal assault that involved sexual abuse. They campaigned successfully against sexual abuse and, in 1908, the first Incest Act was passed. Few prosecutions were carried out under this Act. In its first year, there were 24 cases; by 1920 this had risen to 57. By the 1980s, prosecutions were running at about 500 a year, with a wider social recognition and condemnation of the problem.

Neglect through poor mothering, rather than abuse, was seen as the major cause of death. (Fathers were not expected to care directly, but to earn the money.) Society began to have higher expectations about children's survival. Poor care was not just seen as a sign that the parents were morally depraved nor were deaths tolerated as evidence of Darwin's rule of survival of the fittest. It came to be understood that the quality of mothering mattered and it could be improved by professional help. In 1907, health visiting began with the aim of helping working-class mothers develop good patterns of care. An improvement in general social conditions had the most effect on children's health and survival: with public health measures and a rising standard of living, the child death rate fell over the next three decades.

After World War I, psychology and psychiatry flourished, studying children's development, especially the abnormal, the delinquent and the gifted. Their focus was obviously more on psychological factors than economic. The period saw the start of the Child Guidance Clinics that offered treatment to mothers to improve their care of the child. Infant mortality and juvenile delinquency were of more concern than cruelty to children. There seems to have been low public awareness of male violence to wives or children or, at least, of public condemnation of such violence, and, so, little incentive to investigate or protect abused children.

World War II brought children's conditions to public attention again. The mass evacuation demonstrated to the rural areas quite how extensive urban poverty was and how much it affected the health and behaviour of children. Evacuation also helped people to appreciate the importance of relationships. It suited the politicians to separate mothers and children – putting children in places of safety and freeing the mothers for war work. But they did not like being separated; children were very upset at leaving their mothers. This observation was reinforced by the work of John Bowlby (1953), who developed attachment theory, which stressed the importance of a secure, sensitive relationship in early childhood for a person's development into a happy, well-balanced adult. His ideas came to public attention just after the war when they fitted the political mood of the time and received widespread acceptance. Having encouraged mothers to leave their children to the care of others in order to do war work, politicians now wanted to encourage them back into the home so that jobs were freed for men.

After the war, two major reports led to a reshaping of child welfare services. First, there was major publicity when Dennis O'Neil was killed by his foster father in 1945. There was a public inquiry into the care provided by the local authority and it was found that Dennis and his brother had been placed with foster parents with little assessment of their suitability or subsequent supervision of their treatment of the boys (Home Office, 1945). Secondly, in 1946, the Curtis Report was published, dealing with the conditions of children in care and 'deprived of a normal family life with their own parents and relatives'. These two reports led to the 1948 Children Act, which established Children's Departments and child-care officers with greatly increased responsibility to assess and monitor foster carers.

This Act was passed as part of the creation of the post-war welfare state. It abandoned the stigmatising assumptions of the Poor Law and embodied a far more positive and optimistic view of the family.

> The aim of the 1948 Act was not to punish bad parents but to act in the interests of the children. As the emphasis was on the strength and formative power of the natural family this meant trying to maintain children in the family. It heralded an era where most families were encouraged and helped to care for their own children in their homes, and underlined the importance of both the natural home and the child's own parents to his or her development. (Parton, 1985: 42)

Growing confidence in the possibility, as well as the desirability, of preventing a child's removal from the birth family, led to the 1963 Children and Young Persons Act. This gave local authorities much more extensive duties and powers relating to preventing family breakdown. The childcare service, in theory, should have been shifting from being a last resort for a small number of children from bad homes to a broader and more supportive service aimed at a much wider group.

GROWING SOCIAL AWARENESS OF CHILD ABUSE

The policy of prioritising more supportive work was affected by a growing knowledge that some children suffered terribly at the hands of their parents. The upsurge in public concern about child abuse is usually dated to the work of Kempe, in the 1960s, an American doctor who coined the phrase 'battered baby syndrome' (Kempe et al., 1962). Diagnosis was partly aided by the use of X-rays, enabling doctors to see all the old fractures. X-rays were influential because they provided incontrovertible evidence that the child had suffered injury. Baby battering was seen by Kempe as an illness. In his view, the child needed to be removed from home while the parents received treatment, after which the child could be returned. Parents who had a psychotic illness were not deemed treatable and so their children would need permanent alternative care.

Kempe was a very successful campaigner and he put child abuse on the map in America and, later, in Britain. It is interesting to speculate as to why society should have been willing to listen and why abuse became so politically important. Corby (1987) suggests that the way he classified abuse as a medical condition made it more acceptable for the times and less threatening to the autonomy of the family. The medicalisation of abuse also helped to distance it from its social context and, specifically, from the earlier assumed link with poverty. It could be treated as a health problem, not a social problem, and this was more politically acceptable (Hacking, 1999).

Parton (1985) suggests that child abuse gained so much attention in the 1960s and '70s partly, at least, because it suited the two main professional groups involved with it then. It gave paediatricians an important role in diagnosing this medical condition and it gave the NSPCC a new role. Their work had been taken over, for the most part, by statutory services, and taking up the issue of child abuse gave them a distinctive new contribution to make.

In 1973 Maria Colwell was killed by her stepfather and the subsequent public outcry led to major changes in child welfare services. It might be argued that Maria's case was so influential because her story was so distressing that it forced itself into public awareness. However, Parton (1985) suggests that its significance comes mainly from being at the right time, capturing a public shift in attitudes to the rights and welfare of children. Similar high-profile cases changed public attitudes to child abuse in other developed countries around the same time and this period is marked by an increasing concern to protect children, giving more weight to the rights of the child and less to the rights of parents.

There was extensive media coverage of Maria's death and the history behind it. She had been taken into care when a few months old because of neglect and lived happily with an aunt and uncle. When she was six, her mother who had remarried, applied to have her back. Despite Maria's opposition to the idea, she was returned. It later transpired that, in the thirteen months before she died, she had been cruelly mistreated, starved, and treated as a scapegoat. The post-mortem showed that she had suffered numerous injuries and was well below average weight at her death. The public horror at her story led to an inquiry into the conduct of the professionals involved in her case (DHSS, 1974). As a result of this inquiry, formal procedures were introduced to deal with abuse cases. The three main aims were:

1. To increase awareness of child abuse and professionals' ability to recognise it. Maria's social workers had had little training in the subject and failed to notice classic signs of neglect such as her weight loss or to monitor her progress closely by, for instance, checking with the school.

2. To improve co-operation between professionals because one of the big faults in the Colwell case had been that each professional had some worrying information but it was not shared so the full picture was not seen. This lack of sharing information was a finding of several similar public inquiries in the 1970s.
3. To set up risk registers to improve monitoring so that any professional could easily find out if anyone else had any concerns about the safety of a child.

Maria's social worker was castigated for trying to keep the family together, although this had been the general policy at the time. She was so anxious to try and maintain her relationship with the parents that she was reluctant to challenge them and risk losing their co-operation.

As a result of the Colwell Inquiry, the DHSS came up with guidance, *not* rules, but the clear expectation was that professionals should make the detection of abuse their highest priority. This obviously reduced time and resources for preventive/supportive work since there was no extra cash for this new public concern.

Dingwall et al.'s research, carried out in 1983, suggests that although policy recommended a more intrusive approach, professionals were still reluctant to intervene and operated a 'rule of optimism', looking for the most benign explanation of any signs of abuse and being slow to take action against parents. Professionals were gradually pushed towards a policing approach by continuing media pressure and a series of public inquiries into child deaths. In this series, the death of Jasmine Beckford was particularly significant. In 1984, in circumstances very similar to Maria Colwell's, Jasmine was taken into care after being abused and then was returned to her mother and stepfather. Like Maria, she lost weight steadily at home but her social worker failed to notice or see its significance. She suffered a number of injuries, including a broken leg, before being killed by her stepfather. The public inquiry produced a very emotive report condemning the social workers for putting rehabilitation as their main aim, not the safety of the child (London Borough of Brent, 1985). The report firmly concluded that social workers' primary task was to protect children; the needs and rights of parents should take second place.

The DHSS produced more guidelines supporting this approach and the terminology changed from child abuse to child protection. There was a growing assumption in society that child abuse could be prevented by competent professionals. This is apparent in the media attitude: a child's death was seen more as a failure of the professionals than the fault of the parent who had actually killed the child.

Public inquiries like Beckford's that were critical of professionals got wide coverage while more favourable reports were overlooked. A study of the 45 inquiries conducted between 1973 and 1994, found that 42 per cent were not critical of social workers (and, indeed, many praised the quality of the work) while 25 per cent of reports did not find fault with any professional, concluding that the death was not predictable on the information available (Munro, 1999).

With the pressure on professionals not to miss a single case of abuse, work with children and families became skewed towards investigations of any allegation of abuse (Hill, 1990). This absorbed time and resources and affected the relationship between professionals and families. It also affected the public's view of social work: the control part of their job was more obvious than the care side. This led to a backlash (Myers, 1994) where professionals were seen as becoming too powerful and intervening too readily in the privacy of the family. Myers (1994) gives examples of the emotive language used. The child protection system was described as 'trampling the rights of innocent citizens' and engaging in 'hysterical witch-hunts'; social workers were likened to 'Nazis', 'McCarthyite persecutors' and the KGB.

In England, this public concern came to a head in 1987 when, in Cleveland, there was a sudden surge in the number of children being taken into care because of sexual abuse (Department of Health, 1988). Children taken to a paediatrician for other problems were, to their parents' shock, diagnosed as being the victims of sexual abuse on the basis of a controversial diagnostic test and taken into care. It is still unclear how many cases were falsely diagnosed – although, with hindsight, we know that many were accurate – but the media response expressed the firm view that professionals had got it wrong on a large scale.

The pressure was now on professionals to avoid mistakes of any kind. False accusations were as undesirable as missing a case of serious abuse. In practice, the emphasis was put on ever more thorough investigations in the hope of improving accuracy. The police began to take a leading role and standards of evidence were, in effect, raised from 'the balance of probabilities' to 'beyond reasonable doubt'. Child protection moved, as Parton (1991) points out, from a socio-medical framework to a socio-legal one. Thorpe (1994) graphically describes how the therapeutic orientation of child protection was replaced by 'the forensic gaze'.

Child abuse investigations have come to dominate child welfare services in Britain to such an extent that they swallow up the bulk of resources (Audit Commission, 1994). There is little help available for families experiencing lower levels of difficulties in child rearing – professionals wait until the problems escalate before becoming involved. Ironically, the emphasis on investigation means that there are few services available to families once they are identified as abusive (Farmer and Owen, 1995).

A set of major studies, mostly funded by the Department of Health (1995), have provided detailed evidence of the effects this is having on the experience of families subject to investigation. In the process of detecting true incidents of abuse, large numbers of families suffer the distress of an investigation with no help being offered. Gibbons et al.'s (1995) study found that, for every child placed on the child protection register, six had been investigated and screened out. The focus on risk assessment has led to the family's needs being overlooked. Families' relationships with social workers have changed radically. Where once many families saw them as a source of assistance, most now view them with mistrust. After witnessing the extent of trauma experienced by families and seeing the damage done to longer-term relationships with social workers, Cleaver and Freeman (1995) question whether this is not too high a price to pay for finding the rare cases of serious abuse. The need to alter the present system is now widely recognised (Audit Commission, 1994; Department of Health, 1995; Parton et al., 1997) but solutions are not so clear-cut.

The Audit Commission suggests that professionals should improve the speed and accuracy of their ability to identify high-risk cases so that fewer resources are necessary for this task, freeing money to provide more supportive and preventive services for families. The Department of Health has urged social workers to 'refocus' child protection in the context of children in need, advising them to turn 'investigations' into 'enquiries', and to work in greater harmony with parents, assessing broader family functioning instead of the current narrow focus on risk assessment. Since no extra resources are available, funding for services to meet family needs could be obtained by savings on the number and length of inquiries.

Parton et al. (1997) are very sceptical of the feasibility of the Department of Health's proposals:

> The uncertainties and tensions which current policy debates are attempting to address cannot be changed by remedial action aimed at redefining child protection as child welfare, child abuse as children in need or investigations as inquiries. (1997: 230)

They are critical of the narrow focus on professional practice with too little attention being given to the social context in which the practice occurs. The way child protection work has developed has been strongly influenced by society's views on risk and its expectations of what professionals can or ought to do: 'The contemporary nature of risk in child protection is central' (1997: 232).

The force of this argument can be seen if we look at the recent pressures on child protection professionals in terms of the relative importance society places on false positives and false negatives in assessing the risk of abuse. This analysis helps to emphasise the central role of values in child protection work and how those values are determined by the wider society, not professionals alone.

Since risk assessment is, by definition, making judgements under conditions of uncertainty, there is an unavoidable chance of error. It is impossible to identify infallibly those children who are in serious danger of abuse. Professionals can only make fallible judgements of the probability of abuse. There are, however, two types of error that can be made: false positives and false negatives; that is, some families may be falsely accused

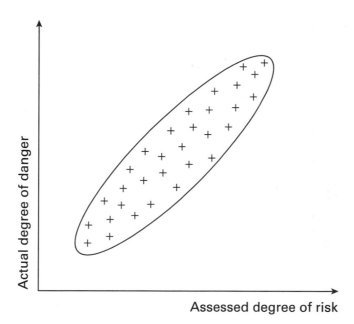

FIGURE 3.1 **High accuracy**

of being dangerous while others are incorrectly cleared. The changes in society's view of child abuse and its expectations of professionals can be expressed in terms of changes in the consensus view on the acceptability of each type of error.

The Taylor-Russell diagram (1939) helps to illustrate the elements involved. The two axes measure the degree of actual abuse and the assessment of risk. If we had a perfect way of identifying high-risk families, we would expect cases to follow a straight line with real and identified risk being the same. However, since we can have only fallible measures, cases will fall within an ellipse, and the less accurate the diagnostic system, the bigger the scatter. Hence, a good diagnostic system would produce a graph like Figure 3.1, while a less accurate one would look like Figure 3.2.

Professionals assessing risk need to make decisions about the threshold for intervention. Once these are added to the picture, the rate of false positives and negatives becomes apparent. A low threshold for intervention produces a high rate of false positives (Figure 3.3) while, conversely, a high threshold leads to a high number of false negatives, of missed cases of serious abuse (Figure 3.4).

The threshold for intervention is a separate decision from the estimation of the probability of a particular outcome. Researchers may help professionals make more accurate estimates but they will not determine the point at which professionals should act. This is a value judgement made

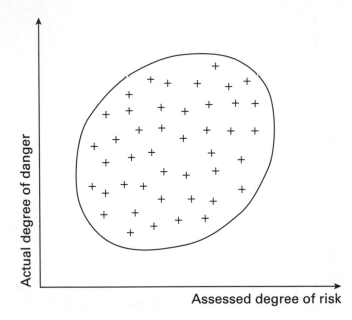

FIGURE 3.2 **Low accuracy**

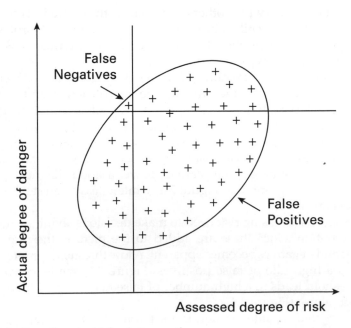

FIGURE 3.3 **Low threshold for intervention**

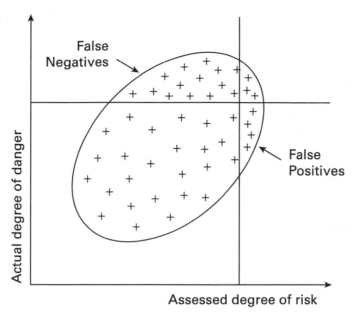

FIGURE 3.4 **High threshold for intervention**

by policy makers and, in recent years, it has been strongly influenced by both media coverage of mistakes and the public's response.

Another crucial point that these diagrams illustrate is that, given the same level of accuracy, moving the threshold to reduce one type of error automatically increases the other type. Thus, in child protection history, when society was outraged by the death of Maria Colwell, professionals responded by lowering the threshold for intervention to minimise the chances of missing another child in such extreme danger. This necessarily led to more families with low *actual* levels of abuse being caught up in the net. The cases of Cleveland and Orkney were unsurprising consequences: on these occasions, professionals were criticised for intervening inappropriately and removing large numbers of children from their homes unnecessarily. These well-publicised cases reinforced a growing public perception that social workers had been given too much power and were misusing it. Another way of describing their actions is to say that they were following the wishes of the general public in trying to avoid overlooking a child in need of protection.

After Cleveland, there was strong pressure to avoid false positives but, unfortunately for professionals, there was no public acceptance of the logical consequence that this would lead to more false negatives and so increase the chances of another tragedy like that of Maria Colwell. Faced with this dilemma, professionals took the only rational course open to them, that of trying to increase the accuracy of identifying high-risk families and so reducing both false positives and false negatives. In terms of the Taylor-Russell diagram, if the ellipse can be made smaller, then both types of error will be less frequent. Investigations therefore became the central task of child protection agencies, with a more thorough and single-minded focus on the risk of abuse to the detriment of assessing the family's other needs and with little attention paid to the costs either to the agency, in terms of resources, or to families, in terms of pain and trauma.

Many have now recognised the faults in the current state of affairs in child protection systems but this situation has come about, I would argue, not from stupidity or carelessness but from a rational attempt to respond to the changing and conflicting demands of society.

CONCLUSION

The work of child protection professionals in helping to reduce the incidence of child abuse and neglect is shaped by the society around them. Although most countries have signed the United Nations Convention on the Rights of the Child, the experience of life for children and parents varies greatly. For some, their society is unable to provide the very basic elements of a safe and healthy childhood. Affluent societies vary the degree to which they believe child rearing is a private matter to be left to parents with minimal state interference and how much responsibility society accepts for creating an environment that supports families and shares the burden. The status given to women and children varies as does the rate of violence generally.

While history shows continual change in societies, the rate of change they are currently experiencing is exceptional. In people's personal lives, the traditional gender roles are being revised so that new family structures and child-rearing styles are burgeoning with, as yet, unknown consequences for the welfare of children. The type of work available and the patterns of our working lives are being transformed, with female participation greatly increased. Demographic changes are altering the shape of society so that the ratio of young to old is decreasing. The autonomy of the nation state is under threat from the forces of globalisation. The widespread rejection of traditional socialism led to neo-liberal politics flourishing in the 1980s and '90s. This politics is now being challenged by new interpretations of left-of-centre values that aim to improve social solidarity and opportunities for all citizens. How this battle will develop is, as yet, unknown but it will have a significant impact on the context of child protection work.

Britain has a long tradition of taking a liberal, individualistic approach. Despite a brief consensus in the post-war decades about funding a universal welfare state, the longer-standing beliefs about family privacy and autonomy and the dangers of encouraging welfare dependency came back to prominence in the 1980s. Welfare services were pared down and increasingly targeted at a stigmatised minority. Poverty, especially childhood poverty, increased dramatically. The Labour government, elected in 1997, has pledged to eliminate child poverty and improve public services but their strategies, so far, are having only slow and small-scale success.

Within child welfare services, specifically, the concerns and priorities of society at large determine the nature of the work. At present, in Britain and other English-speaking countries, the pressures on child protection seem quite irrational and conflicting. There is an overt concern to protect children from all types of abuse but the emotional pressure is to prioritise extremely serious abuse to a degree that has a detrimental effect on every other aspect of the service. The rights of children are more strongly recognised nowadays but society is reluctant to address the complexities of how to respond when their rights conflict with parental rights. Grappling with these inconsistent social demands is a stressful, but inescapable, task for child protection agencies.

SUMMARY

- Protecting children from harm at the hands of their parents and carers occurs within a social context that shapes every stage of the process, from the initial assumptions about what counts as abuse, to professionals' duties and powers to intervene, the options available to them, and the relative desirability of different possible solutions.
- The level of social and economic support for families differs radically between countries. Rates of childhood poverty are particularly varied.
- Child welfare services have the, sometimes conflicting, dual aims of protecting children and supporting families but the relative importance ascribed to each varies over time and between countries.
- In some countries the emphasis placed on accurately identifying high-risk cases is, inadvertently, having a detrimental effect on the rest of child welfare services.

4

defining child abuse

At its simplest, child abuse can be defined as ways of treating a child that are harmful and morally wrong. To call an action abusive is never just a description but also an evaluation. An action can be harmful but morally sanctioned. Many medical practices, for example, involve a degree of harm but are justified by their long-term value to the child. Some religious practices, such as circumcision, involve injury to the child but are defended by certain social groups. Nor does harm refer solely to the physical or psychological effects on the child but can be more intangible. It may include actions that infringe the rights of a child, whether or not this has any perceptible detrimental effect in other ways. The arguments against spanking, for instance, are not based just on a claim that corporal punishment has a long-term damaging impact but, irrespective of its effect, it can be condemned as treating children with less than the rights they deserve.

Definitions of abuse, therefore, embody beliefs about what child rearing behaviour is unacceptable or dangerous and values about people: the relative rights of adults and children, the relative value of males and females. Hence, there is considerable variation over time and between cultures in what is deemed abusive. It is hard to find any universal agreement on precise behaviours that are abusive. Killing children might seem an obvious candidate for an extreme form of physical abuse but it is not always condemned in all societies. In many societies, male babies are more highly valued because they will remain within the family group as adults and look after their parents in old age. The birth of female babies, therefore, can be a disappointment and they are vulnerable to socially tolerated killings. 'In Bangladesh, India and Pakistan ... a million girls die each year because they are born female' (UNICEF, 1992).

There are also a number of practices in the world that seem harmful to the children involved and yet are widespread in their societies. Child labour, sometimes in conditions amounting to slavery and often for long hours and in dangerously unhealthy conditions, is commonplace in some developing countries (Seabrook, 2001). In some societies, fathers may sell their daughters into brothels for the sake of improving the economic status of the rest of the family. Institutional care for children can be of an appalling standard that threatens their prospects of healthy development (UNICEF, 1997).

This lack of consensus creates major problems for the study of child abuse. The core concept is ambiguous, contested, and shifting. But the concept of abuse is still problematic even when a consensus can be reached. Since the subject matter is intentional human behaviour, it is not possible to specify abuse just in behavioural terms. It also includes some comparison with a standard of acceptable parenting and some comment on what was going on in the mind of the abuser. A degree of intuitive appraisal is therefore essential. Progress can and has been made within particular social groups in developing public criteria for identifying abuse but this progress falls short of removing the human interpreter of behaviour. This chapter examines the implications this has for research, policy and practice. It begins with a critical look at a sample of definitions and discusses the feasibility of developing more precision. Many people have described the term 'child abuse' as 'socially constructed' but what does this add to our understanding? An analysis of the debate finds that, for many, it is only a rephrasing of the point that beliefs and values are important in its definition. For others, the phrase is the trigger for an exploration of the power issues involved: which sections of society are constructing it and should it be reconstructed in ways that empower other sections? The final part of the chapter discusses the repercussions for research, policy, and practice of dealing with such an imprecise concept.

SAMPLE DEFINITIONS

At an international level, countries have been able to find a formulation that allows them to agree on condemning child abuse. Article 19 of the 1989 United Nations Convention on the Rights of the Child defines it as:

> All forms of physical or mental violence, injury or abuse, neglect or negligent treatment, maltreatment or exploitation, including sexual abuse.

In looking at other attempts at general definitions, the same lack of precision is found but what is also found is that, over time, the concept has been expanded from an initial concern with serious physical cruelty and neglect. The first British legislation specifically addressing child abuse, the 1889 Prevention of Cruelty to, and Better Protection of, Children Act, defined cruelty in the following context:

> Any person, over sixteen years of age who, having the custody, control or charge of a child, being a boy under the age of fourteen years, or being a girl under the age of sixteen years, wilfully ill-treats, neglects, abandons, or exposes such child, or causes or procures such child to be ill-treated, neglected, abandoned, or exposed, in a manner likely to cause such child unnecessary suffering, or injury to its health. (1889 Prevention of Cruelty to Children Act, Ch. 44)

In the 1960s, the pioneering work of Kempe in the USA brought the concept of child abuse to public notice but his original concept was relatively precisely defined and linked to repeated physical abuse of a degree that caused fractured bones. This degree of assault was clearly outside the usual level of injury caused by physical chastisement at that time in the USA. Since the 1960s, however, the concept has been made ever broader (Parton et al., 1997). It quickly expanded to include neglect, which can have equally devastating physical effects on the child, but has subsequently come to cover psychological harm and sexual abuse. Research evidence (Gibbons et al., 1995b) suggests that psychological abuse may, in fact, have the most serious long-term repercussions for the victim (assuming that the victims of physical harm survive the immediate injuries). It is, though, one of the hardest on which to reach agreement.

This widening of the meaning of child abuse means that, for some, it has become equated with all acts or omissions that hamper a child's development. The leading international journal on child abuse: *Child Abuse and Neglect: The International Journal*, defined its aims as

> providing an international multidisciplinary forum on all aspects of child abuse and neglect including sexual abuse, with special emphasis on prevention and treatment. The scope extends to all those aspects of life which either favour or hinder optimal family interaction. (ISPCAN, 1994)

The British National Commission of Inquiry into the Prevention of Child Abuse adopted an even broader definition, taking its scope outside the family:

> Child abuse consists of anything which individuals, institutions, or processes do or fail to do which directly or indirectly harms children or damages their prospects of safe and healthy development into adulthood. (National Commission, 1996: 2)

This includes abuse by systems: systems abuse can be said to occur whenever the operation of legislation, officially sanctioned procedures or operational practices within systems or institutions is avoidably damaging to children and their families.

This final definition clearly goes far beyond the remit of any child protection agency. The focus of child welfare and child protection services is typically on the harm children may suffer at the hands of their parents or carers, rather than on the damage done by wider aspects of society. Therefore, in looking at the problems of defining abuse, this is the area I shall focus on.

Problems arise as soon as an attempt is made to go beyond these general formulations that are, largely, statements of good intent more than serious attempts to define the problem. The National Research Council in the USA summed up the results of efforts to develop more precise specifications of abuse:

Despite vigorous debate over the last two decades, little progress has been made in constructing clear, reliable, valid and useful definitions of child abuse and neglect.... The vagueness and ambiguities that surround the definition of this particular problem touch every aspect of the field – reporting system, treatment programs, research and policy planning. (National Research Council, 1993: 57)

Individual societies are able to supply slightly more detailed definitions of what abuse means within their legal system. In Britain, the Department of Health and Social Security (1988) provides the following specification, using what are now widely taken as the standard four sub-categories of abuse:

Physical Abuse

Physical abuse may involve hitting, shaking, throwing, poisoning, burning or scalding, drowning, suffocating, or otherwise causing physical harm to a child. 'Munchausen syndrome by proxy' may also constitute physical abuse, whereby a parent or carer feigns the symptoms of, or deliberately causes ill health in, a child.

Emotional Abuse

Emotional abuse is the persistent emotional ill-treatment of a child such as to cause severe and persistent adverse effects on the child's emotional development. It may involve conveying to children that they are worthless or unloved, inadequate, or valued only in so far as they meet the needs of another person. It may involve causing children frequently to feel frightened or in danger, or the exploitation or corruption of children. Some level of emotional abuse is involved in all types of ill-treatment of a child, though it may occur alone.

Sexual Abuse

Sexual abuse involves forcing or enticing a child or young person to take part in sexual activities, whether or not the child is aware of what is happening. The activities may involve physical contact, including penetrative or non-penetrative acts. They may include non-contact activities, such as involving children in looking at pornographic material or watching sexual activities, or encouraging children to behave in sexually inappropriate ways.

Neglect

Neglect is the persistent failure to meet a child's basic physical and psychological needs, likely to result in the serious impairment of the child's health or development. It may involve a parent or carer failing to provide adequate food, shelter and clothing, failing to protect a child from physical harm or danger, or failing to ensure access to appropriate medical care or treatment. It may also include neglect of a child's basic emotional needs.

While this set of definitions is far more specific than the earlier ones quoted, it still does not reduce the concept to behaviour alone. There is frequent use of the word 'may' and this is unavoidable. The behaviours that 'may' be abusive can also occur in contexts where they are interpreted in a more benign way.

There are two problems in trying to reduce 'abuse' to specific behaviours. Firstly, the centrality of beliefs and values about child rearing makes it very hard to reach a precise agreement on what is unacceptable or dangerous care. In Britain, for instance, the majority of parents will use some degree of physical chastisement but they will differ in what they consider acceptable. The amount of force used, the age, strength and gender of the child, will all influence their individual judgements on what is or is not acceptable. Secondly, the meaning of any behaviour depends on the overall context. For instance:

- Hitting a child on the back because he is choking is a different action from the same behaviour done with the intention of hurting him. Failing to give a child sufficient food because there is a famine in his or her country is not condemned as parental abuse although the same behaviour in Britain would be. The essential role of interpretation in making sense of human actions means that, even when a social group can agree on quite specific rules of care, there is still a place for intuitive appraisal of whether any one instance should be seen as abusive.
- Penetrative sex with a three-year-old girl would be reasonably uncontroversial as a precise behaviour that is an instance of sexual abuse in Britain but difficulties arise when dealing with teenage girls. Should we specify the legal age of consent – sixteen years – as the age below which the definition applies or should we try to take account of the physical and emotional maturity of the girl and the age the man believed her to be? In Britain, indeed, under-age sex is dealt with in remarkably different ways. A fourteen-year-old girl who is found by the police soliciting as a prostitute will be seen as a criminal whereas a girl of the same age who is found by Social Services to be having intercourse with her elder brother will be classed as a victim of abuse.
- Emotional abuse is even more problematic. The upper classes in Britain have long had a tradition of sending their children to boarding schools, sometimes at as young an age as five. To many others, this seems likely to have a harmful effect on the child's emotional development.
- Parents influence a child's behaviour with a mixture of positive reinforcement and punishment but the relative amount of each varies along a continuum. Parents at one extreme think other, less punitive, parents

are at risk of spoiling the child while, in turn, they are criticised for using a harmful level of chastisement.

- Parents have widely varying views on how much supervision is needed. A degree of freedom that, to one parent, is encouraging the child's independence is seen by another as grossly neglectful, exposing the child to danger.

All parents are imperfect to some degree so any single item of abusive behaviour will be found from time to time in most families. It is the intensity and the chronicity of the behaviour that cause damage.

In practice, within a particular society, it is usually possible to reach a high degree of agreement about the most serious instances of abuse although there is considerable scope for dispute about lesser forms. Chastising a child so ferociously that the child is severely brain damaged would be universally condemned as abusive in Britain nowadays. (It was explicitly permitted in law in the eighteenth century. Even causing death while punishing a child was classed as a misadventure [Jones, 1945: 10]). The problem in this instance is more likely to be establishing that the injuries were non-accidental, i.e. clarifying the perpetrator's motives.

To some extent, differences of belief about how to care for children may be reduced by long-term research that demonstrates the impact of different styles of parenting. In Britain, the Department of Health believes that such research will significantly lessen the scope for controversy (1995). However, there are reasons for caution about this. Firstly, there are immense methodological problems in identifying reliably the impact of specific variables on child development. So many variables are involved that very large samples are needed to tease out the influence of any one factor. Secondly, the research assumes a consensus on what a healthy adult looks like. This is far from being the case. The issue is particularly apparent in relation to gender issues where social expectations are changing rapidly (Giddens, 1999). How assertive or submissive should a girl be? Is aggression wholly wrong? Should she be dependent on male decision-making or think for herself? For men too, the swift rate of change in contemporary society is raising questions about what type of man will flourish. Should parents encourage a son to hide his feelings so that he appears tough or should he be allowed to be as sensitive as his sister? Should he be prepared to fight or are verbal and relationship skills more important?

Gabarino (1992: 158) makes the valuable point that over the last two decades there have been dramatic changes in mainstream (i.e. middle-class) attitudes and behaviours in relation to child rearing; for instance, there is growing opposition to hitting children, while increased importance is attached to cognitive development and educational achievement. So, as middle-class views are dominant in society, the benchmark against which abuse is measured is changing.

In the natural sciences, concept definition often goes hand in hand with theory development. As the theory explains a concept, it becomes possible to say more and more precisely what the exact boundaries of the concept are. Once scientists had developed a theory of light, for example, it became possible to define different colours very precisely in terms of their wavelengths. It is possible that similar progress will be made in child abuse research at least in relation to particular sub-categories of abuse. Studies of persistent paedophilia, for instance, might yield a clearer formulation of the motivation behind it. This, in turn, might predict specific ways it shows in behaviour.

At present, however, the theoretical scene is confusing. There are three main approaches to theorising about abuse: the medical, the legal and the sociological. In the 1960s, Kempe presented it as a product of parental illness, with an emphasis on diagnosis and treatment. In legal circles, it is seen as a crime, with the focus being on investigation, prosecution and punishment of the offender. To a sociologist, it is a form of social deviance presenting issues in understanding the social factors that encourage it, and devising means of controlling it. Each approach generates different types of hypotheses and uses different research methods to test them.

THE SOCIAL CONSTRUCTION OF CHILD ABUSE

Discussions about the problem of defining abuse are often linked to debates about social construction. Child abuse is frequently described as a 'socially constructed' concept. Since Gelles (1975) first made this claim, it has become widely accepted (Parton, 1985; Department of Health, 1995). What does this mean?

It does not mean that the behaviour described as child abuse was *created* by society. The concept of child abuse has a very recent history. Kempe's work in the 1960s can be seen as the major starting point. Yet we clearly want to be able to say that children suffered at the hands of their carers before we developed the modern terminology of child abuse and neglect. A child in the fifteenth century whose bones were broken by an angry father suffered the same type of pain as a child in the twenty-first century. Rape causes injury and distress to a three-year-old girl, regardless of the period of history into which she was born. It is not the behaviour that is socially constructed but the way we talk about it. Previous generations talked of cruelty and incest where we talk about abuse. There is some common ground in what the various terms – cruelty, abuse, battered babies – are referring to but they have different connotations.

If all that the concept of social construction adds to the debate is to draw attention to the role of beliefs and values in our understanding of abuse, what is the point of highlighting it?

Why Social Construction?

At one level, the idea of social construction is uncontroversial. It points to the way that a concept is 'a product of historical events, social forces and ideology' (Hacking, 1999: 2). It is not ordained by the nature of the world but, given different forces at work, could have been (and in the case of child abuse, has been) seen differently. The Department of Health, when describing child abuse as socially constructed, seems to use it in this very moderate way with little practical significance except to acknowledge that values play a part in the definition.

If this is uncontroversial, why has talk of social construction become so widespread? Hacking (1999: 6) argues that most people who talk of the social construction of a concept 'want to criticise, change or destroy' it: a socially constructed concept can be *reconstructed*. The key message in discussions of social construction is that the concept is not fixed and immutable for all time. Therefore, it is worth analysing how the concept was shaped and moulded with a view to altering it or promoting a rival interpretation.

If we look at child abuse literature, we see two distinct schools of thought about the role of social forces in shaping the concept of abuse. There are those who, while acknowledging the difficulties in reaching a clear and precise definition, nevertheless assume that there is some social consensus about what is, or is not, abusive behaviour and that there is some single entity or process that can be studied and explained. For these, the main problems arise in delineating the boundaries rather than the central features of abuse. The National Research Council's (1993) impressive review of child abuse theory, research and practice in the USA falls into this category. It recognises the ambiguity of the concept, the probable complexity of its causation, and the difficulty of intervening effectively, but it also sees it as a subject for scientific research that can be generalised to other countries. The obstacles to a universal theory of causation and cure are described in terms of research problems: the difficulties of developing valid instruments, of collecting data with high inter-rater reliability, and of isolating the effect of different variables that tend to co-exist. The Department of Health's (1995) summary of research on the working of the British child protection system takes a similar line despite making an overt reference to social construction, citing Gibbons et al.'s (1995b) description of child abuse:

> As a phenomenon, child maltreatment is more like pornography than whooping cough. It is a socially constructed phenomenon which reflects values and opinions of a particular culture at a particular time.

In the Department of Health's research review, child abuse is presented as being on a continuum from acceptable to unacceptable forms of child rearing and the main problem highlighted is that of thresholds for action. How unacceptable does behaviour need to be before social intervention is warranted? The lower the threshold, the more families will be classed as abusive. This idea of a continuum, while having much practical merit, still involves the assumption that there is some agreement about what is desirable or undesirable, with most of the disputes centred on when to intervene. The dominant message in this discussion of defining abuse is that the problem will eventually be eased, if not resolved, by research that identifies what child-rearing practices are harmful to children. Therefore, it offers the hope that there can be some value neutral and consensual definition once enough research has been carried out.

This low-key approach to the significance of social construction is opposed by those who highlight the role of power in shaping society's perception of abuse. It is not just that the concept is shaped and moulded by the values and opinions of a society but also that these values are the dominant ones and the power base of child abuse needs to be examined and critiqued.

One line of argument is that, in developed countries, abuse is being presented as a defect of parenting, as essentially an individual responsibility and failing. So, covertly, attention is distracted from the wider social forces that can make it harder to be a good parent – primarily, poverty.

As mentioned in Chapter 3, in Victorian England, early legislation on child cruelty was applied almost entirely to the poor. Referrals to the National Society for the Prevention of Cruelty to Children (NSPCC) centred on the working class, the main cause for concern being neglect in households with very low incomes, and only 7–10 per cent of referrals concerned ill-treatment. One characteristic of the development of the concept in recent decades is that it has been distanced from poverty. Kempe, in the 1960s, presented it as an illness that was found in all classes. This distancing has become very apparent in the last two decades in the USA and Britain where child poverty has been increasing rapidly (Piachaud and Sutherland, 2000).

Beard (1990) questions why public concern is directed toward individual abusers:

> For all its horror, child sexual abuse [or physical battering] harms, indeed kills, far fewer children, either in the UK or the US, than simple, miserable and unremitting poverty. Why, when poverty has been intensifying and welfare programmes run down, has our attention been drawn to sexual or other abuse?

It is clear, from the statistics, that the majority of families known to child protection and welfare services are poor, and the majority of children who are identified as victims of abuse and neglect are poor (Department of Health, 1995). The causal link could be that parents who are bad at earning money are also bad at caring for their children. But common sense suggests that the causal connection is likely to be the opposite: bringing up children with few material resources and constant financial worries is harder than doing so in affluent, secure surroundings.

Another aspect of the way the concept has been constructed is that it has obscured whose values are being used as the basis for a consensus. While there is clearly considerable variety in beliefs and values about

TABLE 4.1 **Child abuse referral rates in the USA**

	Referral rates
1967–68	7,000
1974	60,000
1982	1.1 million
1989	2.4 million

childcare, any child protection system adopts one set of beliefs and values as the core ones. The Department of Health acknowledges that any definition has to be linked to local values but then assumes that, within Britain, there is a clear consensus. This takes attention away from the fact that it is essentially white, middle-class values that are taken as central. This discriminates not only against the poor but also against ethnic minorities and new forms of family life. There is an overrepresentation of Afro-Caribbean families and single mothers in the British child protection system. The way the issue is currently presented by official bodies obscures the need for the value base to be made explicit and justified.

THE CONSEQUENCES OF PROBLEMS IN DEFINING ABUSE

The difficulties of establishing an agreed definition of child abuse and of specifying any definition in a way that removes the need for individual judgement has serious implications in all areas of research, policy and practice.

Research efforts to study it within a scientific framework are hampered by the variability of the key concepts. Even attempts to get an idea of the size of the problem are complicated. There will always be difficulties in finding out about the incidence of an activity that people want to conceal. Abusive parents are unlikely to be fully frank and honest about their actions. Victims, as well, may have reasons for withholding the truth. But variations in the definitions used also lead to disparities in research findings. Epidemiological studies of the prevalence of child sexual abuse in different countries produced results ranging from 7 per cent to 36 per cent among girls and 3 per cent and 29 per cent among boys (Finkelhor, 1994). In studies in which similar definitions were used, the findings were also comparable, suggesting that the gross disparities between some of the other studies were mainly due to definitional differences.

Hacking (1999: 143) uses the American example of the number of children referred to child protection services to illustrate the variation in reported incidence. Hacking then demonstrates how difficult it is to separate the relative contributions of definitional variation and reporting variation to the gross differences. The rate of referral to the US services rose rapidly in recent decades (see Table 4.1).

Clearly, some of the rise in referrals is due to increased public knowledge and concern for abused children. But to what extent is the increase due to a broadening definition of abuse so that more parenting behaviour is categorised as abusive? Widening the definition of abuse suggests that standards of childcare are rising and behaviour once tolerated is now being condemned. However, the rising statistics could indicate the opposite, that there is a rise in the number of children actually being abused. If this were so, it would be a matter of grave concern, but, given the softness of the data, it is impossible to determine whether or not there is an underlying trend of increasing harm to children or of rising standards of care.

Definition problems also hamper the use of research findings. As was mentioned in Chapter 2 in relation to the finding on the abusiveness of stepfathers, it is problematic to generalise from one country to another and it can also be problematic within the same country if researchers have used slightly different definitions. For the purposes of research, it may be possible to develop a standardised operational definition in relation to a small category of abuse, such as sexual abuse that includes penetration. Researchers can choose to concentrate on one area, unlike practitioners who have to respond to all referrals sent to them. However, even with an operational definition, there tend to be some less clear-cut elements such as the context, the cultural meaning, and the long-term pattern of behaviour. Therefore, training is needed to create a group of observers who will apply the concept in a consistent way.

In practice, many researchers rely on case records and the judgements of practitioners for their data. This means that there is likely to be considerable variation in how intuitive judgements have been reached and this causes problems for generalising about research findings.

Definitional problems have implications for policy makers. In general, policy makers would not be expected to use very precise terms. In talking of health policy, for instance, they leave the detailed classification of illness and treatment to the medical profession. The same applies to child protection policy but the lack of professional consensus in how to interpret policy then produces problems. In Britain, research has revealed that, despite a common policy, there is enormous variation in how it is implemented throughout the country (Gibbons et al., 1995a). The rates of referral and of investigations, the numbers of children on the 'At Risk Register', and the numbers of children removed from their parents all vary considerably around the country. The statistics also reveal an over-representation of certain groups. Afro-Caribbean families appear more frequently than expected, even if we allow for economic factors. Single mothers also receive more attention than seems warranted. The English law refers to the concept of 'significant harm' and, while it is easy at one level to understand what is meant, it is not easy to specify at a more detailed level so that it will be consistently applied throughout the country. This raises serious questions about justice. The aim is to provide an equitable service. Parents in the north of the country should be treated in the same way as those in the south; black families should receive the same response as white for similar behaviour.

For practitioners, the difficuly of clearly defining 'abuse' increases the responsibility on them to make judgements in each case. They face two layers of problems. Firstly, there are many practical problems in establishing precisely what has happened to a referred child. Since abuse does not simply refer to observable behaviour but to actions, practitioners have to interpret the intentions behind the actions, using their knowledge of the overall context and their folk psychology. Secondly, there are the problems of deciding whether the action(s) should be classified as abusive and, if so, how serious they are.

It is not usually left to one individual to judge an action but that action is discussed by the professional group and with the family. Professionals, in general, try to act in accordance with the dominant values in society rather than by imposing their personal beliefs on families.

The increasing ethnic diversity in modern societies creates dilemmas for professionals, who have to learn how to make sense of actions within the family's cultural context as well as judging them by the standards of the wider society. The perplexity that professionals can feel when dealing with a new ethnic group illustrates the importance of background knowledge, of folk psychology, in our everyday lives. When we do not understand the broad cultural context of behaviour, we can feel at a loss as to how to react. Yet family life is an area where cultural beliefs, values and attitudes are of great significance, influencing all members' roles, their interrelationships, and their relationships to the outside world. Even when we have made sense of a family's actions, the question can arise of how much we can tolerate behaviour towards a child in an ethnic community that would be condemned if it were found in other groups in society. This is an ethical dilemma that is often met in practice and to which there is no easy answer.

There is some evidence that professionals are affected by their exposure to problem families so that they, unwittingly, start to tolerate as acceptable a lower standard than the rest of society. In the USA, Rose and Meezan (1996) compared the views of social workers and mothers from the local area on what level of care amounted to neglect and found that the mothers had much higher standards than the social workers. They also found that mothers from ethnic minorities had higher standards than native white Americans.

CONCLUSION

Definitions of child abuse depend on our beliefs about acceptable and unacceptable ways of treating children. Social groups change their beliefs about standards of childcare over time and there are considerable differences between groups. Historically, it seems, societies first become concerned about protecting children from serious physical injury and neglect. At a later stage, they become aware of, and condemn, child sexual abuse and, then, extend their concern to include emotional abuse. There has also been a broadening of each category of abuse so that it is not just the most serious levels that are condemned.

The history of child protection agencies offers a very positive picture of societies gradually giving children more rights and wanting a higher and higher quality of life for them. At a global level, however, it needs to be remembered how many children are dying in wars, famines and droughts, dying from treatable diseases, and dying because they are the 'wrong' gender. There are also numerous others living in dangerous circumstances, being exploited in the labour market or the sex industry, or cared for in institutions where their basic needs are not met. Their suffering cannot be relieved by child protection agencies but it is salutary to remember that the harm caused by parents and carers is only one type of abuse that children endure.

It is not just the changing nature of the concept of abuse that causes problems for research and practice. There is also the difficulty of defining it so precisely that agreement is reached on which actions are abusive and how serious they are. There is then the difficulty of deciding, in a particular instance, whether the observed behaviour is an action of the type we consider abusive. These issues cause major problems for building up a knowledge base with universal relevance.

For practitioners, the complexity of the concept of abuse presents daily dilemmas in deciding how to categorise referrals. A good degree of consensus about standards can be developed in a particular social setting, especially in classifying what counts as serious abuse. However, as beliefs about good child-rearing practices are continually evolving, there will always be a need for an ongoing discussion about the boundaries of acceptable and unacceptable behaviour. Even when there is consensus on standards, life is not simple for practitioners since they still have to make sense of the behaviour reported to them and interpret what type of action it is. The growth of ethnic diversity in modern societies has highlighted the importance of people's background knowledge in understanding each other. When practitioners and policy makers lack that broad understanding, they have great difficulty in knowing how to classify people's actions.

SUMMARY

- Describing an action as abusive always includes a moral judgement.
- There is no universal consensus on definition except at the most abstract level.
- Research studies use different definitions, making it hard to generalise from one study to another and from one country to another.
- In practice, professionals are faced more often with dilemmas about *how* abusive an action is, and what level of response from themselves it warrants.

5

the difficulties of assessing risk

The language of risk is new to child protection work. In childcare textbooks from the 1950s or '60s, there was no reference to risk assessments. Indeed, even the term 'child abuse' was rare. The language was more in terms of child concerns, child welfare, and child well-being. The parents were not abusers but problem families, dysfunctional families, and parents in need of help. To a worker in 1960, an assessment would have meant an assessment of family functioning to see how well the child's needs were being met, not an assessment of risk.

Introducing the term 'risk' shifts the emphasis from the here and now to the future. A risk assessment makes a prediction about what might happen to the child. Given the limited knowledge base, these predictions are always couched in terms of probabilities: there is a certain degree of risk of some event happening. Risk assessment, therefore, involves computing and combining probabilities. The formal laws for doing this are expressed in probability theory. Unfortunately, humans are not good at dealing with probabilities intuitively. People's instinctive understanding of how probabilities should behave is wildly wrong, resulting in persistent and fundamental mistakes. The topic of risk assessment is, therefore, one where the conflict between the analytic and intuitive approaches is in full cry, and is manifest in the dispute between actuarial and clinical risk assessments. It seems to be an area where more formal methods are crucial to counterbalance the flaws of the human mind. Paul Meehl, an eminent psychologist, argues that we should be ready to acknowledge our intuitive weaknesses in this area:

> Surely we all know that the human brain is poor at weighing and computing. When you check out at a supermarket, you don't eyeball the heap of purchases and say to the clerk, 'Well it looks to me as if it's about $17.00 worth; what do you think?' The clerk adds it up. (Meehl, 1986: 372)

The clerk would not hesitate to use an adding machine and would, indeed, be expected to do so. Asking a child protection worker to collect an array of risk factors and weigh them is a similar task, so the use of aids to compute probabilities should be equally acceptable.

These comments indicate that I think that formal analysis of probabilities has a great advantage over intuition. However, the practical implications of this are not straightforward. This and the following chapter are both concerned with risk assessment but, while the next chapter looks at the practice issues, this chapter is more abstract. It aims to explain the basics of probability theory to show what is involved in trying to identify risk factors and in developing instruments for predicting risk. The sections detailing the background mathematics can be omitted by those whose main interest is in the discussion.

The main lesson to learn from a study of the mathematics of prediction is how difficult it is to develop any predictive instrument with a high degree of accuracy in child protection. Admitting that actuarial systems are so inadequate is not an argument for preferring clinical judgements: there are overwhelming arguments for accepting that the latter are probably far less accurate. They are certainly no more accurate. Acceptance of the limits of our predictive ability should, instead, make us argue for realistic professional aspirations, resisting the understandable, but impossible, social pressures put on child protection workers to be fortune-tellers. The scope for inaccurate judgements, of both overestimating and underestimating danger, is so great that it must form a part of the planning in case management.

Another lesson that can be drawn from studying the formal process of risk assessment is how small an element of practice it, in fact, encompasses. Once the risk has been assessed, the more substantial task is to manage it, to think of how to intervene to reduce it. This requires a far broader assessment of the family and the circumstances.

WHAT IS RISK?

Risk is an ambiguous and confusing concept. It has two significantly different meanings and the one you choose to use has a pervasive impact on your subsequent thinking. Historically, the 'risk' of a certain outcome referred only to the probability of its happening; the term was neutral about whether that outcome was desirable or not. Hence, in a card game, there is the risk both of winning and of losing a fortune. The weather forecast might indicate a risk of rain or of sunshine. Currently it is most often associated with unwanted outcomes only; in child protection work, people talk of the risk of harm to a child but not of the risk of a happy childhood. In discussions of 'the risk society' (Beck, 1992; Giddens, 1990), the assumption is that we are talking about undesirable results. This shift in meaning is perhaps so far advanced that it is useless to go against the tide and use the term in its former, neutral, sense. However, the focus on the negative distorts reality and, in child protection, can lead to a skewed picture of practice. Child protection workers have a duty to promote children's welfare as well as protect them, to *maximise* their well-being as well as to *minimise* any danger. They cannot just work to avoid risk. For instance, they never face a choice between a safe and a risky option. All the possible avenues hold some dangers and they involve making complex assessments, balancing risks and deciding on the safest path. Also, and of equal importance, all of the options contain some good aspects, some benefits for the child, and these have to be weighed against the dangers. A classic scenario involves choosing between leaving children in their birth family or moving them to a new home. The final decision on what to do will be based on an assessment of the strengths as well as the weaknesses of the family, what the children may lose as well as gain by leaving, and what problems and advantages they might face in a foster home.

The shift in recent decades that has put talk of *risk* assessment and *risk* management at the top of the agenda has distracted attention from the central purpose of a child protection system, which is not just to keep children alive but to maximise their welfare. Risk is only one component in the assessment of a family that is needed to decide whether or how to intervene. The later part of this chapter considers how much has changed in child protection by moving to the language of risk.

HOW NOVEL IS RISK ASSESSMENT?

Recent changes in child protection have involved not just the introduction of the language of risk but also the concept of abuse. A risk assessment aims to predict the probability of a child's suffering from abuse if the situation continues unaltered. The concept of abuse has also undergone change, expanding from its early definition of severe physical abuse or extreme neglect to cover any action or omission by parents that may have an adverse effect on a child's development. Both these developments have to be borne in mind when considering how the modern risk assessment differs, if at all, from the type of family assessment that would have been conducted in the past. A child welfare worker in the 1960s would have been concerned with whether the child's needs were being met. 'Risk' and 'need', in the context of child abuse, can be defined in terms of each other. If a child's needs are not met, there is a risk of harm. If a child is at risk of abuse, then he or she is in danger of not having some needs met.

The difference, if any, between the new and old style assessments seems to be in the time span they are concerned with. Because of the expansion in the meaning of 'abuse', risk assessment can refer to two crucially different processes. The first, and possibly the one the public would instinctively think of, is assessing the *immediate* danger to the child. If an allegation of abuse is made to a child protection agency, the first response has to be whether the information indicates that this type of risk assessment must be done. The second meaning of 'risk assessment' is broader, deriving from the expansion in meaning of the term 'abuse' to include all forms of adverse parenting. Will the child suffer detrimental effects on development in the long term?

The distinction between immediate and long-term risk correlates, to some degree, with different types of abuse. Serious physical and sexual abuse carries a clearer risk of short-term harm whereas psychological abuse and all but the most extreme forms of neglect present less urgent problems. With these forms of persistent abuse, it is the cumulative effect that causes the damage to the child's development and research suggests that the damage can be severe:

> Long-term problems occur when *the parenting style* fails to compensate for the inevitable deficiencies that become manifest in the course of the 20 years or so it takes to bring up a child. During this period, occasional neglect, unnecessary or severe punishment or some form of family discord can be expected. ... If parenting is entirely negative, it will be damaging; if negative events are interspersed with positive experiences, outcomes will be better.... In families low on warmth and high on criticism, negative incidents accumulate as if to remind a child that he or she is unloved. (Department of Health, 1995: 19)

In Britain, the assessment of immediate risk has become dominant with unintended consequences. Agencies faced with a steep increase in allegations of abuse combined with limited resources had to make decisions about priorities. The political and social pressures to prevent child death or serious injury have placed the forms of abuse that carry immediate danger higher on the agenda than the types of chronic abuse that produce serious problems for children in the long term. Hence, physical and sexual abuse and extreme neglect are more often the focus of intervention than psychological abuse and lower-level neglect, although evidence suggests that the latter is extremely harmful to children's development (Egeland and Sroufe, 1981 and 1983; Gibbons et al., 1995b). To the public, the causal links between chronic abuse and problems in adult life are not so apparent and so do not spark such concern as do the clear injuries of physical and sexual abuse.

The focus on short-term risks has determined not only which families get close attention but also where that attention is focused: on the immediate dangers to the child. Research by the Department of Health (1995) found that many of the families who were assessed appeared to experience significant long-term problems in caring for their children adequately but were offered no services unless there was also immediate risk.

In Britain, concern with the skewed emphasis on investigation and attention to immediate risk led to a 'refocusing' policy where greater attention was to be paid to assessing the level of family functioning and whether the needs of the child are being met (Department of Health, 1995). This policy presents children at risk (needing immediate protection) as a sub-group of children in need (whose parents are not providing adequate care in some respect). They can, however, just as easily all be categorised as children at risk, with some at risk of immediate harm and others at risk of long-term harm.

It is a matter for politicians to decide what risks to a child their country's child protection agencies should prioritise, but the experience in Britain shows how a shift in emphasis can have quite unintended consequences for practice.

The narrow risk assessment has an essential role in front-line work but, even with cases of immediate danger, it is not generally adequate on its own. The broader family assessment is needed as the basis for planning and intervention. Even in extreme cases where the risk is clearly so high that the child has to be removed instantly, longer-term decisions about the feasibility of rehabilitation require a thorough assessment of the family.

The distinction between a narrow risk assessment, concerned primarily with predicting short-term harm, and an assessment of family functioning, concerned with long-term harm, needs to be kept in mind in this and the following chapter, as I look at research on risk assessment and the process of conducting a risk assessment.

WHAT IS A RISK FACTOR?

A risk factor for abuse is a feature found more often in abusive families than in the general population. Intuitively, people tend to think that the more frequently a factor is found in abusive families, the stronger it predicts risk, but this is incorrect. The crucial point is how common it is *relative to* its general incidence. Poverty is a common feature of abusive families but this, on its own, is not enough information to use as a predictor. In Britain in 2001, around 21 per cent of children were living in poverty, so, to determine how strong a predictor of abuse poverty is, we would also need to know its precise incidence in abusive families. If only around a fifth of children known to have been abused are poor, it has no predictive value at all. If a much higher percentage are poor it is a strong predictor; if a lower percentage are poor, it is a contraindication.

How strongly a risk factor predicts the undesired outcome – in this case, abuse – depends on two variables: how common the factor is in the sub-group of families that are abusive and how common it is in the population at large (the base rate). Figures 5.1–5.4 show how these two variables can combine and the effect this has on predictive value.

Figure 5.1 illustrates a factor that has no predictive power because it occurs as commonly in the general population as in the sub-group of abusers.

At the other extreme, Figure 5.2 shows how a factor could be such a strong predictor that it is diagnostic of abuse. It is not found at all in the non-abusive population and is found in *all* abusers. Finding such a powerful

Same incidence in general and abusive populations

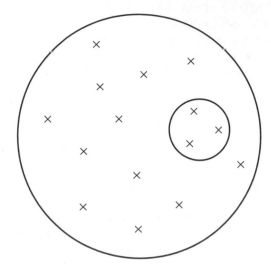

FIGURE 5.1 **No predictive value**

Factor only found in abusive population and all
abusers have it

FIGURE 5.2 **Completely predictive of abuse**

Very, very rare in general population and much more
common, though still rare, in the abusing population

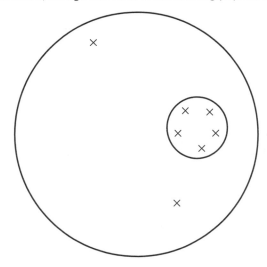

FIGURE 5.3 **Highly predictive of abuse**

predictor would be ideal, making professional assessment of risk immea-
surably simpler. Medicine provides some examples of such success.
Doctors have been able to identify symptoms that are found in all and
only the people with a particular disease, enabling them to develop diagnostic tests that are highly accurate. For example, a particular type of
abnormal blood culture indicates bacteraemia. It is unrealistic to expect
similar success in relation to predicting abuse since it differs significantly
from an infectious disease. As discussed earlier, the basic concept is so
ambiguous and covers such a range of behaviours, it is unlikely to have
one common causation or common marker.

A factor may be rare among abusers but, because it is even rarer in the
general population, can be highly predictive.

The most common type of risk factor that research has been able to
identify is much weaker; something that is fairly common in general but
slightly higher in the abusive population. Although this strength of risk
factor has some predictive value, Figure 5.4 illustrates an important point:
the factor is fairly common in both abusive and non-abusive families;
since the sub-group of abusers is such a small percentage of the total
population, most families where the factor is found will be non-abusive.
For example, some research has reported that stepfathers are more likely
to be abusive than birth fathers but, even if this is true, the majority of
stepfathers will not be abusers and the majority of male abusers will not
be stepfathers.

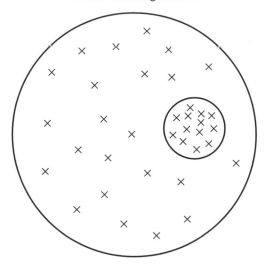

Fairly common in the general population but more
common among abusers

FIGURE 5.4 **Moderate predictive value**

Professionals cannot rely on practical experience to identify risk factors
or to work out how common they are in either the general population or
among abusers. Indeed, their practice is likely to give them a biased view
of human nature since they have relatively little professional experience
of happy, non-problematic families. They also tend to get biased feedback.
If they *underestimate* the risk to a child, they are likely to realise their error
when the child is injured. If they *overestimate* it, however, they will probably take steps to 'protect' the child and prevent injury; the fact that the
child is then not injured will not make them question their judgement.

A recent review of research (Hagall, 1998) produced the following findings on predictors of physical violence (see Table 5.1).

ACTUARIAL AND CLINICAL RISK ASSESSMENT

How can knowledge about predictors of abuse be used? The literature
offers two competing models: clinical and actuarial prediction. Grove and
Meehl (1996) provide the following definitions:

An actuarial assessment 'involves a formal, algorithmic, objective procedure
(e.g. equation) to reach the decision'. (1996: 293)

A clinical assessment 'relies on an informal, "in the head", impressionistic, subjective conclusion reached (somehow) by a human clinical judge. (1996: 294)

TABLE 5.1 **Perpetrator-based risk indicators for dangerousness**

Factors where research evidence is fairly clear that the risks of violence, at least, are increased:

- a record of previous violence;
- level of previous offending of any type;
- being male;
- having a history of past mental health problems, particularly if hospitalised;
- personality disorder;
- non-compliance (particularly with medication);
- personal history of abuse or neglect;
- cognitive distortions concerning the use of violence.

Factors where research evidence is equivocal or insufficient:

- use and availability of weapons;
- substance abuse;
- current psychiatric symptomatology;
- misperceptions about child behaviour.

In no case is the relationship absolute, or the mediator and mechanisms clear.

Victim and situational risk factors

Risk factors relating to the victim:

- being young (under 5, particularly);
- being premature, or of low birth weight;
- being more difficult to control;
- giving an account of harm or danger.

Risk factors associated with the situation:

- family problems;
- low levels of social support;
- high levels of socio-economic stress;
- access to the child;
- organisational dangerousness and poor decision making.

From A. Hagall (1998) *Dangerous Care: Reviewing the Risks to Children from Their Carers.* London: Bridge Child Care Consultancy.

The reader can probably guess from the wording of these two definitions that the authors are strongly in favour of actuarial assessment schedules. They also pose the choice between the models as a very stark dichotomy, reflecting a similarly absolute view on the difference between analytic and intuitive thinking. In reality, child protection offers a range of aids to risk assessment that vary on two points: what type of information is collected and how it is weighed. In terms of the evidence they use, they vary between employing simple observation or professional expertise in deciding whether the factors are present. For example, details of a criminal record can be ascertained by reading the relevant files; but the quality of the parent/child attachment requires professional judgement. Also, instruments compute the factors differently. Most use clinical judgement, requiring the professional to make an intuitive appraisal of the range of information collected. In an actuarial instrument, however, all the evidence is given some numerical rating and the answer is reached by using some statistical formula. It is, therefore, more useful to think of risk assessment instruments as providing a more or less structured approach to collecting information, and an intuitive or formal method of interpreting it.

I want to look at the current and potential strengths of actuarial instruments before considering their limitations. Grove and Meehl's enthusiasm for actuarial predictions is based on good grounds. In areas where such tools have been developed and evaluated, they demonstrate a higher level of accuracy and consistency than professional judgements. Grove and Meehl report a meta-analysis of 136 studies that compared clinical and actuarial prediction in psychology and medicine. Only eight showed the clinical predictions as superior; in 64, actuarial prediction was more accurate; and in the remaining 64, there was no significant difference between the two.

In looking at how actuarial predictions are made, it is easy to see why they could be expected to be more accurate and consistent than clinical prediction. First, consider how they are developed. There are two sources of information to identify what factors to include. One strategy is to conduct empirical research on the general and the abusive populations to get the figures to fit into Venn diagrams like the ones in Figures 5.1–5.4, making it possible to work out how strong a predictor a factor is. Alternatively, a group of experts in the field can meet to identify the factors they have found to be significant. Evidence suggests that this latter method is the most frequently used in developing child protection instruments (Keller et al., 1988). The type of data collected by an actuarial risk instrument can be quantitative or qualitative; it can require simple observation or expert professional judgement.

It is not how the information is gathered that makes it an actuarial approach but how it is then dealt with. Statistics, not intuition, are used to reach the answer. It is a formal method of doing what the clinician is trying to do informally. The Venn diagrams in Figures 5.1–5.4 illustrate how a factor's predictive strength can be worked out. It is not easy to do this intuitively with just one factor; in a risk assessment, there are several factors to consider at the same time. To repeat the analogy I used in the introduction to this chapter, the task is at least as difficult as trying to estimate the cost of a basket of shopping by just looking at it. There is a wealth of psychology research on the errors of clinical judgement (Nisbett and Ross, 1980; Meehl, 1992; Plous, 1993). The actuarial instrument takes the best evidence available and formally applies the statistical formulae that the clinician is using informally and, probably, inaccurately.

There is a lot of resistance to actuarial methods in the helping professions. Some dislike its mechanical dimension. However, it should be remembered that the only mechanical part is in computing the evidence, not in dealing with the family. The way evidence is collected requires the usual relationship and investigation skills. There is nothing in the use of actuarial instruments that requires the professional to be non-empathic or cold. In the hands of a poor practitioner it can, of course, be used in this way as a means of avoiding involvement. Poor interviewing skills, however, are likely to lead to poor data collection and, so, make the instrument less accurate.

Another argument against actuarial methods is that, sometimes, the professional knows some details about a family that are so unusual that they will not have been taken into account in actuarial research. It is claimed that, in such cases, professionals are right to jettison the actuarial prediction and rely on their own. Frederick and Rosemary West could be such a case. They were a British couple found guilty of sexually abusing numerous women & girls and killing twelve, including two of their own children. Frederick committed suicide on conviction but his wife is still in prison. When she is released, no child protection service would fail to intervene if they found she was taking care of any child. Yet, actuarial systems cannot have included in their data serial killers because they are, fortunately, so rare. The weakness with this argument for exceptional cases is that professionals may know that some features are rare but this rarity in itself means that they have little experience to go on and, in most cases, are only able to guess at their significance in relation to abusiveness.

Having praised the reliability of actuarial methods in *principle*, I now want to consider their value in child protection *practice*, first looking at the evidence on the currently available instruments, and, second, clarifying the precise role they can play in the overall management of a child abuse case.

EVALUATING RISK ASSESSMENT INSTRUMENTS

The first point is that assessment instruments need to be evaluated. However they are drawn up, it is necessary to check how they perform in practice. Moreover, it is not possible to buy a tested actuarial instrument off the shelf unless it has been evaluated on a group of people similar to the group on which it will be used. Therefore, there are restrictions on adopting instruments developed in other countries without further research. In addition, the research needs to look at both accuracy and inter-user consistency, and it needs to compare the accuracy with the professional judgements it might be used to replace to provide persuasive evidence that it would be worth adopting the instrument.

In this section, I will detail how to evaluate the accuracy of a risk assessment instrument because it is complicated and it is also counter-intuitive. For those readers who are not interested in the underlying mathematics and want to move on to the next section, the crucial message is that it is surprisingly hard to develop a high accuracy rate in predicting a relatively rare event. Even instruments with what seem to be impressively high statistics about how many families they will accurately identify as abusive or safe have a disappointingly low overall accuracy: the majority of the families the instrument identifies as abusive will, in fact, be non-abusive, that is, they will be false positives.

Sometimes, writers make the claim that a particular assessment method has an accuracy rate of, say, 65 per cent. People, understandably, often think this means that 65 per cent of positive identifications will be accurate. This is not the case. From this one statistic alone, it is impossible to work out how useful the method will be in practice. The values of three variables are needed:

Sensitivity: how many cases of abuse it will predict accurately (true positives)
Specificity: how many non-abusive families it will identify correctly (true negatives)
Base rate or prevalence of the phenomenon: how common is it in the population in general.

Bayes's theorem (Bayes, 1763) can be used to calculate the positive predictive value of the test – the probability that a family that is identified by the test or risk instrument will actually be abusive. If the probability of abuse is p(a), and the probability of being identified as abusive is p(t), then p(a/t) is the variable we want to work out – the probability that abuse will occur in a family identified as abusive (the probability of a prediction of abuse being a true positive).

The first step is to work out the overall probability of getting a positive result from the instrument. This is where common sense tends to be wrong; people think that a high specificity produces a low rate of positive results. Since a high specificity means that the instrument will correctly identify most *non-abusive* families and most families in the population are non-abusive, intuitively it seems that only a few families will be identified as abusive. However, this is wrong. The prevalence of abuse has to be included in the calculations and this leads to a strikingly different outcome.

To make the maths simpler, let us suppose that the rate of abuse is one in a hundred. (Estimates of abuse vary widely, depending on the definitions used. Child protection services are generally only concerned with the more serious forms of abuse and so the rate is likely to be fairly low. Basically, the lower the incidence, the harder it is to make accurate predictions.) Let us assume too that the instrument has a very good specificity (95 per cent) and sensitivity (90 per cent). If the instrument is used on a 100 families, there is a 90 per cent probability that it will identify the one expected true case of an abusive family (remember the prevalence is said to be 1 in 100). But the specificity, although high, has an error rate of 5 per cent so the instrument will also identify 5 per cent of the 99 safe families as abusive. Thus the total number of positive results will be

$$(0.01 \times 0.9) + (0.05 \times 0.99) = 0.009 + 0.0495$$

so the probability of getting a positive result on the instrument when it is used on a family is p(0.0585).

If the instrument has been used and the family has been identified as abusive, how likely is this to be accurate? (This is the accuracy rate needed to guide our confidence in practice.) This is where Bayes's theorem applies:

$$P(a/t) = \frac{\text{sensitivity} \times \text{prevalence}}{\text{probability of a positive result}} = \frac{p(t/a)\,p(a)}{p(t)}$$

In this example, the calculation is:

$$P(a/t) = \frac{1 \times 0.01}{0.0585} = 0.15$$

This means that there is only a probability of 0.15 that a family identified as abusive will actually be so. If you get a positive result on 100 families, 15 will be accurately identified and the vast majority – 85 – will be falsely identified; they will not be a danger to their children.

In reality, accuracy rates are even worse than this because no instrument claims anything approaching such high sensitivity or specificity as I have assumed here. Accuracy, however, crucially depends also on the prevalence of the predicted factor and so instruments will vary depending on what population they have been developed for. If the aim is to develop a screening method to use on all families, then the statistics to use must be based on the general population, and within this group, the prevalence of serious abuse is fairly low from a statistical point of view, making accurate prediction extremely difficult. However, if the goal is to devise a way of identifying high-risk families from the population of families known to child protection services as having already been abusive to some degree, then instruments dealing with this calculation can realistically expect to achieve much higher levels of accuracy because of the greater prevalence of abuse of within these families. If the calculations above were repeated and we assume that one in five families known to child protection would reabuse, then the total number of positive results would be:

$$(0.2 \times 0.9) + (0.05 \times 0.8) = 0.18 + 0.04$$

making the probability of getting a positive result when the instrument is used p(0.22). Bayes's theorem would then be:

$$P(a/t) - \frac{1 \times 0.2}{0.22} = 0.9$$

So, in this case, if it is predicted that 100 families will reabuse, 90 of the predictions will be accurate and only 10 families will be falsely identified.

To summarise, the accuracy of any predictive system depends on its sensitivity (the rate of true positives), its specificity (the rate of true negatives) and the base rate (how common the predicted factor is in the population). People tend to forget the importance of finding out the base rate although, as the examples above have shown, it has an over-whelming impact on the overall accuracy. In this instance, probability theory conflicts sharply with intuitive reasoning. A famous study, 'The Harvard Medical School Test', illustrates the prevalence of the intuitive bias in evaluating predictive tests. Staff and students at Harvard Medical School were told of a diagnostic test that had a high sensitivity of 95 per cent and a superb specificity of 100 per cent (no one with the disease would test negative). They were asked the probability of some-one who tested positive actually having the disease. The majority of respondents gave the answer of 0.95 – the rate of true positives – over-looking the significance of the base rate in determining the accuracy (Casscells et al., 1978). Depending on whether the illness being diag-nosed was common or rare, this test might or might not be clinically valuable.

CURRENT RISK ASSESSMENT INSTRUMENTS

What levels of accuracy have existing instruments been able to achieve? There have been some American reviews of current studies (Johnson, 1996; Lyons et al., 1996). The authors comment that most of the instru-ments in use in the USA have not been empirically validated. In review-ing the evaluations that have been carried out, they list the specificity and sensitivity, but not the prevalence rates, so that the reader is unable to judge their overall accuracy. Accuracy has been measured in terms of being better than chance but another omission in the research is that it is rarely checked against clinical assessments. This information is vital if a case is to be made for introducing them since a major reason would be that, however imperfect, instruments are superior to professional judgement.

Although not providing all the answers needed, these studies do provide some interesting details of how risk assessment instruments are being developed. The majority derive from expert opinion and a literature review rather than empirical studies of the prevalence of factors among abusers and the general population. In particular, there is a lack of empirical study of the factors that predict reabuse. Since there seems no convincing reason for supposing that the same factors predict a single case of abuse and repeated abusive behaviour, this area of research is vital in developing instruments to help professionals with the decision on which families already known to child protection services need to be followed up.

Perhaps because of the reliance on expert opinion, the instruments do not have much in common. The number of factors listed ranges from 5 to 13. No factor appears in every instrument but perpetrator access and the age or ability of the child are the most frequently found factors. Another limitation in current instruments is that all except one claim to predict all forms of abuse. (The exception predicts physical abuse only.) Again, it seems dubious to assume that all types of abuse will occur in families with similar features. Sexual and physical abuse, for instance, would at first glance appear to result from somewhat different pathways.

Another issue that is being increasingly recognised as essential in evaluating risk assessment instruments is their cultural sensitivity. What ethnic group have they been tested on and is the same accuracy achieved when used on other groups? There are many reasons for supposing that ethnicity will affect professionals' interpretation of family behaviour and that factors that correlate with abuse in one group may not do so in another cultural context. Single parenthood, for instance, has different social consequences in different groups and, therefore, it might be expected to lead to varying degrees or types of stresses on the parent.

One of the main arguments offered by agencies for introducing risk assessment instruments is that they increase consistency across the agency and, so, offer a more equitable service to families. To test this, studies have to measure the degree of inter-user agreement. Results so far provide good support for the claim that instruments improve consistency between workers.

A final aspect is how much impact they actually make on practice. The results of studies are scarce but disappointing. One such study (Fluke et al., 1993) found their use made little difference to the type of decisions made and that half the staff used them *after* they had reached a decision. There was a general sense that risk assessment was largely peripheral to their work with clients. Another survey of 328 child protection workers in the USA reported that 75 per cent of respondents thought using risk assessment instruments increased their workloads with little benefit. Only 14 per cent thought their use was 'very important' (American Humane Association, 1993).

What conclusions can be drawn from these studies? One is that more research needs to be done. All of the topics I have mentioned merit scrutiny and have, as yet, been inadequately examined. There are many different aspects that need to be looked at to provide a detailed picture of how the instruments work in practice and so help determine whether they should be more widely incorporated into practice.

Further cause for concern is the depressing level of accuracy they have. Some writers have argued that this evidence is grounds for practitioners' reluctance to use them and continuing to rely on clinical judgement (Sargent in Parsloe, 1999; Department of Health, 2001). Yet there is no reason to have greater confidence in clinical judgement. It is not that research has shown it to be superior; it is just that the relevant research is lacking to evaluate it. There seems no good reason to suppose that practitioners can do better than statistical prediction. There are several reasons to expect them to be worse.

Problems with Intuitive Assessment

First, all the reasons why it is difficult to identify strong predictive risk factors apply as much to intuitive practice wisdom as to empirical research. Second, most of the risk instruments are based on expert opinions on what factors should be included so they are using the same body of knowledge as the experts; the only difference between the formal instrument and the expert clinical judgement is that the instrument carries out the statistical computations using formulae and does not rely on people's notoriously poor intuitive handling of the task. Third and finally, experience gives practitioners a very limited and biased set of information about abusive and non-abusive families. They are not in a position to work out the base rates of any factor in the general population. When reviewing the accuracy of their assessments, they get biased feedback. If they have predicted a high probability of risk, then they will have intervened to lower it. If the family then do not abuse, professionals do not know whether it is the result of their intervention or of a false risk assessment. However, if a low risk of abuse was predicted, they will also get imperfect feedback. The family may lose contact with the agency and so professionals miss instances of further abuse. Even if the family are re-referred, the professional who made the first assessment may not hear about it. From this it is clear that people's ability to learn from experience is seriously flawed. Empirical research is needed to get a more reliable picture.

Overall, actuarial instruments seem to have great potential for assisting professionals in making assessments of risk by providing a formal means of computing the best available evidence on risk factors. However, they require very extensive testing before they can be relied upon. They also play only a small part in the overall management of a case, providing a judgement about the probability of harm at a particular point in time. As

FIGURE 5.5 **Pushing a rock up a hill**

the next chapter analyses, this is just one component in the total process of risk management.

REVISING RISK ASSESSMENTS

Another way in which the formal laws of probability differ radically from intuitive reasoning is in how assessments are revised in the light of new information. People tend to treat all new evidence in the same way whatever their current risk assessment but, according to probability theory, the current risk assessment affects the impact a new piece of evidence has. Put briefly, if you already consider there to be a high probability of danger, new and compelling information increases the probability only a little; if it's low, then it increases it a lot.

It is like a rock being pushed up a hill that begins with a gentle slope but then gets steeper (Figure 5.5). A small amount of energy will move it a long way on the lower slopes but more and more energy is needed to push the rock higher up the slope. Similarly, when coming down, a small push at the top of the slope will create a big move while greater effort is needed for the final downward stretch. Imagine that the top of the hill signifies certainty that the child is in serious danger while the bottom of the hill equals safety for the child. Learning something new and worrying about the family should alter the estimation of how risky the situation is. However, if the child is already thought to be at high risk (near the top of the hill), the assessment should be increased only slightly, whereas if the child is considered fairly safe (on the lower slopes), the assessment should be increased more substantially.

Again, for readers who are not interested in the maths behind this account of revising assessments, the following section can be omitted. In explaining Bayes's theorem, I am not suggesting that professionals should necessarily try and use it formally or that calculators and mathematical formulae should become standard features of case conferences. Understanding the formal rules of probability helps professionals understand how their intuitive response is likely to be inaccurate and to adapt accordingly. In particular, it helps to avoid the common bias of intuitive reasoning, which treats new evidence as having equal impact regardless of how high or low the current risk assessment is.

In probability terms, the existing risk assessment is called the prior probability. The concept of the 'prior probability' refers to the intuitive appraisal a professional makes in assessing a case. This judgement is subjective though it is far from being random; it is influenced by research findings, theoretical knowledge and the wisdom acquired through experience. In probability theory, probabilities are assigned a number between zero and one. One equals 100 per cent probability, that is, certainty, and zero is 0 per cent probability, that is, impossibility. A highly likely outcome might be 0.8 and an improbable one 0.1. Professionals in child protection already communicate how serious they think a case is but usually in words rather than figures. Some attempt to estimate the probability of risk to the child is an essential part of practice.

Since the prior probability is a subjective judgement, there is no one objectively right value to assign. This is reflected in practice where professionals may have sharply conflicting views of how risky a situation is and all believe that their own judgement is soundly based. Differences of opinion, however, should lessen if professionals followed probability rules in revising their judgements as new evidence emerges. New information that makes the risk seem higher will have a differential impact on the current assessments so that the gap between them will diminish.

In practical terms, suppose at a pre-birth case conference on a baby, the health visitor believes there is a low risk of abuse but the social worker thinks there is a high risk. The baby is then born prematurely, a known risk factor for being abused. According to probability theory, the new information should increase the social worker's risk assessment only slightly but should have a marked effect on the health visitor's appraisal, bringing the two of them closer together. As further investigations are done, conflicting views should converge more and more. Differences of opinion may, however, remain and these can be perfectly rational because of the subjective elements in risk assessment.

Having covered the central concepts of calculating risk, Bayes's theorem can again be used to calculate the probability of a hypothesis in the light of new information. The three probabilities I have discussed above are:

P(a) – the prior probability; this is the existing estimate of (a) – the risk of abuse.

P(e/a) – how strongly is the new piece of evidence (e) linked with abuse – is it found in many or just a few abusing families?

P(e) – how common is that factor in the general population – the base rate.

In Bayes's theorem, the 'posterior probability' (P(a/e) – the revised assessment of risk in the light of new evidence – is calculated on the basis of these probabilities. A formal version of Bayes's theorem, if *a* stands for abuse and *e* for evidence, is as follows:

$$P(a/e) = \frac{P(a)}{P(a) + \dfrac{P(e/\text{not } a)P(\text{not } a)}{P(e/a)}}$$

(See Howson and Urbach (1989) *Scientific Reasoning, The Bayesian Approach.*)

Returning to the example of a health visitor and social worker disagreeing in their risk assessments prior to the birth and responding to the new evidence that the baby was premature, let me provide some figures so that the theorem can be worked out. I will assume that the health visitor expresses her low assessment (the prior probability) as .2, and the social worker's higher one is rated as .8. Klein and Stern (1971) report that 24 per cent of the abused children in their sample were premature, compared with a general rate of 7.5 per cent, so the p(e/a) = .24 and the p(e) = .075. For the health visitor, Bayes's theorem estimates the revised assessment of risk as:

$$P(a/e) = \frac{P(.2)}{P(.2) + \dfrac{P(.075)P(.8)}{P(.24)}}$$

$$= .44$$

Whereas for the social worker, the revised estimate is

$$P(a/e) = \frac{P(.8)}{P(.8) + \dfrac{P(.075)P(.2)}{P(.24)}}$$

$$= .93$$

Although still far apart in their estimates, the two professionals are getting closer. As more and more information is gathered, the discrepancy between them should reduce even further.

CONCLUSION

This chapter has been looking at how difficult it is to predict future harm to a child. Understanding of the causes of abuse is insufficient to identify strong predictors of abusive parents. At best, research has found some data that correlate moderately with a higher chance of being abusive. When it comes to using these research findings, professionals have a choice of an actuarial or clinical way of computing their findings. I have argued that there are good reasons for supposing that actuarial risk instruments will be more useful than leaving this difficult judgement to intuitive appraisal alone. However, such instruments are not a simple solution. They require extensive testing of their accuracy relative both to chance and to clinical judgement, their cultural sensitivity, and their relevance to a specific population.

At best, an actuarial instrument will help in making a judgement about the level of risk to a child in a particular family at a particular time. Risk assessment is an ongoing not a once-in-a-lifetime matter. Families and their circumstances change and so their dangerousness alters. Indeed, if the family was seen as high risk, professionals will have been trying to change things so that a revised risk assessment is an essential element of ongoing work with a family. Revising probabilities is counter-intuitive. It depends on how-risky the family is thought to be. New worrying information about a high-risk family pushes the risk up only slightly while the same worrying information learned about a safer family increases the risk assessment much more.

It would appear that the overwhelming message from the discussion of the difficulties of accurate risk assessment is that child protection workers should be very cautious in their claims to be able to predict abuse. This has implications for any message conveyed to politicians and the general public about their skills. The medical profession has clear standards of reasonable practice, and as long as a doctor meets these, he or she will not be castigated for fallibility. Similar standards need to be developed in child protection work so that practitioners can feel confident in making defensible risk assessments. They can never make a 'right' assessment in the sense of an infallibly correct prediction about the future. They can, however, be 'right' in the sense that, on the basis of the evidence they had at the time, this was a reasonable estimate.

Accepting the fallibility of risk assessments has implications for how cases are conducted. It encourages more caution in subsequent work with the family, not only being open to revising the judgement of risk in the light of new evidence but also trying consciously to check the assessment by seeking out that evidence.

SUMMARY

- A risk assessment refers to a specific time frame. In child protection work, a focus on assessing immediate harm can skew practice so that the longer-term risks are ignored or undervalued.
- An item of information is called a risk factor for abuse if it is found more often in abusive families than in the general population. It may be rare among abusive families but, because it is even rarer in the general population, it is still predictive.
- An actuarial risk assessment instrument provides a statistical formula for working out the final risk assessment. A clinical risk assessment relies on the intuitive expertise of the professional, though this can be based on a more or less structured guide to collecting the relevant information.
- With any predictive system, the practitioner wants to know the probability that any particular family it identifies as abusive will actually be so. To determine this, three variables are needed: the sensitivity (the rate of true positives), the specificity (the rate of true negatives), and the incidence of abuse (the base rate).
- The rarer the event to be predicted, the harder it is to develop an instrument with a high rate of accuracy.
- The way new evidence affects a risk assessment depends on how high or low that assessment is. If the current assessment is high, new adverse information increases the probability only a little, whereas if it is low, it increases it more substantially.

6

the process of assessing risk

Complex judgements like risk assessments become easier to handle if they can be analysed into smaller stages. This means the information can be organised in a more accessible manner and be examined at each step in turn so that it is more public and open to debate and review. The process I describe here is very logical and orderly but, in real life, thinking is not so tidy. Information about a family is received in a haphazard and disorganised way. Often a judgement has to be made before all the details are known. Sometimes unexpected information suddenly turns up, forcing a review of the judgement. The jumble of facts, opinions and fears that is the typical content of a child abuse investigation has to have an order imposed on it; the alternative is that professionals become paralysed by the confusion. The formal framework serves this purpose.

The structure I present is a component of the decision-making framework used in the next chapter but, in this chapter, it deals solely with the issue of making a judgement about the degree of risk of abuse. Risk *management*, the subject of the following chapter, is a later stage concerned with making decisions on how to intervene to alter the predicted course of events and so reduce the risk.

THE STAGES OF ASSESSING RISK

1. What is or has been happening?
2. What might happen?
3. How likely are these outcomes
4. How undesirable are they?
5. The overall judgement of risk – a combination of the likelihood and the seriousness.

This framework helps to make explicit the distinction between the likelihood and the undesirability of an outcome. One case may present a high risk of chronic low-level neglect while another poses a low risk but one of a very serious outcome such as death. How these are computed and compared rests on the values and goals of the professionals and families involved. When a judgement is made about the risk, the next stage involves thinking about what can be done to reduce the risk.

With this framework, it can be seen that, in practice, the term 'risk' is so loosely used that it can refer to any of the final four stages of a risk assessment. People discussing a child protection case may say there is a risk of the child's being abused, meaning there is a chance of this happening. They might refer to the risk of death or serious injury, meaning the consequence of being abused and how undesirable it is. It can be unclear whether a case assessed as 'high risk' is one with a high chance of some abuse or with some chance of serious abuse. Risk is also used when talking of the overall likelihood of the adverse outcome, and in computing both its probability and its undesirability. These ambiguities lead to confusion and misunderstanding. Therefore, I shall avoid the word 'risk' except in relation to the overall risk assessment (the result of combining probability and severity), using the more specific terms for the earlier stages of reasoning.

Stage 1: What Is or Has Been Happening?

This question is deceptively simple. It can be answered at many different levels of complexity, from a simple description of behaviour to a comprehensive assessment of how a family is functioning. It is also the most important component of a risk assessment for two reasons. First, the best guide to future behaviour is past behaviour. The family's way of behaving to date is the strongest evidence of how they are likely to behave in the future. Second, professionals are rarely criticised for making poor predictions per se but for making poor assessments of what is or has been happening to the child. Predictions made on the basis of poor assessments are, inevitably, poor quality. Hence, examining this question occupies most of this chapter.

The level at which professionals try to establish what is happening depends, to a large extent, on what practice question they are trying to answer as they progress through a case. The following four questions occur at key stages in practice, depending on how far a case progresses.

1. *What does the referrer claim is happening?* This is linked to the practice question, 'Is this a child protection issue needing some response?'
2. *What do the family and relevant others say is happening in relation to the allegation?* The related practice question is, 'Is the allegation substantiated and/or is there cause for concern?' This focused investigation of the area of behaviour causing concern contributes to decisions about whether there is an issue of concern and whether a broader assessment is needed.
3. *What is happening in this family at a wider level; that is, what is the context in which the alleged abusive behaviour is happening?* This links to the question: 'Do professionals need to intervene?' It identifies what is

going satisfactorily as well as badly in the family and produces a broader picture of how adequate the child care is, helping professionals decide whether they need to intervene.

4. *Why is this happening? What are the causal factors that seem to be con-tributing to the undesirable behaviour?* The practice question is, 'How should professionals intervene?' What can be done to alter the situation so that the level of care improves?

INTUITIVE UNDERSTANDING OF BEHAVIOUR

In trying to answer these questions, the issues raised in Chapter 2 about understanding human behaviour become relevant. Accounts of what is happening draw on some combination of intuitive understanding and explanatory theories, depending on the approach taken by the professionals. Indeed, intuition has an irreplaceable role in making sense of the basic data in a child protection case: the alleged actions or omissions of the abuser. When it comes to human actions, it is not enough just to provide a description of behaviour. An interpretation of what the behaviour means to the actor is needed. Pushing a needle into a child's arm to cause pain is abusive but a doctor pushing a needle into the arm in order to vaccinate the child is not being abusive. The behaviours are similar but, because the intentions of the actors are not the same, they are described as different actions. This feature of understanding people means that, even when everyone involved in a case can agree on what has happened at the behavioural level, they may disagree about what type of action it was.

Intuitive understanding enables us to make sense of behaviour at a basic level, whether or not it can later be explained in terms of some formal theory. Experience, both of life in general and child protection work in particular, helps develop background knowledge about how people tend to behave and why. This introduces a number of problems in practice: there can be disagreement among professionals about how to interpret the observed behaviour; there can be a blurring of facts and values; and all this highlights the importance of understanding a family's culture.

Intuitive understanding works reasonably well in many contexts, and, most of the time, people can reach agreement about the basic actions in a referral. However, because professionals will have slightly different sets of background knowledge, they do not always agree. To one professional, a parent's getting angry at being investigated is the understandable response of an innocent person being wrongly accused; to another, it can seem a sign of guilt. One person may think a slap is a mother disciplining her child appropriately; another may see it as the mother venting her rage and being abusive.

This latter example illustrates another feature of intuitive understanding. Interpretations of behaviour often take the form of tacitly saying whether they are instances of 'normal' parenting or not. But the alternative to 'normal' is rarely 'abnormal' in the sense of pathological, such as an actively psychotic mother disembowelling her baby to placate the voices that are tormenting her. Nor does 'normal' simply refer to the dominant form of behaviour. In any society, there are many different styles of 'normal' parenting. In child protection work, 'normal' means 'acceptable' and 'socially tolerated'. It is contrasted with 'bad'; it is a moral judgement, criticising the parents for acting in a way that is disapproved of. Parton et al.'s (1997) analysis of how duty workers dealt with initial referrals demonstrated the extent to which investigations involve moral judgements of family life.

Most professionals strive not to let their personal values dominate their practice but try to judge families in relation to their social group. This emphasises the importance of understanding the cultural context of families. With increasing ethnic diversity in many countries, child protection agencies are well aware of the need to develop their understanding of the belief systems and values of the families they meet. The range of cross-cultural variability in child-rearing beliefs and behaviours makes it clear that there is no universal standard of optimal childcare or definition of abuse and neglect.

Cultural diversity raises the difficult question of how morally relative a child protection agency can be. An aspect of childcare may be standard or at least condoned within one culture, but can professionals always accept it? There is little problem in tolerating different diets or clothing. But what of differences that are actively condemned if carried out by the majority ethnic group? Different attitudes to issues such as ways of disciplining children, the role of women, or homosexuality cause major problems with no easy solutions. Society wants to respect people's value systems but, at the same time, wants children to experience the same level of protection (Korbin, 1991).

This is not just an issue between groups at different stages of economic development. Conflicting values occur throughout the world. Two neighbouring tribes in Zaire have radically different views on how to treat teenage boys. The Bantu have initiation ceremonies for boys involving circumcision, deprivation of food and sleep, and frequent beatings. Their neighbours, the Mbuti, think this is abusive and terrible and have no comparable initiation rites. But the Bantu think the Mbuti teenagers are also abused because, unless they go through the rites, they cannot be considered adults and so they are being deprived of an essential step in life (Korbin, 1991).

Ignorance of a family's culture may distort our understanding of their behaviour but so may racism. In Britain, there is clear evidence of discrimination against black people in employment, housing and access to social services (Modood and Berthoud, 1997). Within child welfare, there is an overrepresentation of black children in public care and evidence that they come into care more quickly while black parents are less likely to be offered family support services (Barn, 1990; Chand, 2000).

TABLE 6.1 A comparison of significant variations between responses

Action	Unspecified %	Black family %
Initial focus child abuse issues	37.9	56.5
Non-specific concern	35.6	50.6
Discuss with management/specialist	11.5	16.5
Initiate help (not explicitly child protection)	31	20
Initial focus on helping mother	17.2	23.5

One study of professional practice found clear evidence of racism affecting the assessment of risk. Birchall and Hallet (1995: 154) gave this brief vignette to 170 professionals representing the groups involved in child protection:

> In the course of your duties, you hear that a neighbour has said the six-month-old baby next door has chilblains on her hands and is often crying. The mother is a nineteen-year-old and also has a toddler. She lives on Social Security and her fuel has been cut off. You later learn that the baby is below the third centile in weight and height. The mother says she is difficult to feed and is anxious about her. She is clean but has a sore bottom. The toddler is robust though not very warmly dressed. He is very active and rather rough with his toys and his mother.

In half the cases, the family was described as Afro-Caribbean. There were significant differences in the responses of the two groups in Table 6.1.

These findings echo results from the USA: there is a greater readiness to label a case involving a black family as suspected abuse and fewer proposals of direct help or medical attention. Professionals proposed more reference to social work agencies than to medical help.

False assumptions about ethnic groups that present a positive image of them can be just as damaging as negative ones. The inquiry into one child death in England blamed inverse racism for the social workers' overestimating the capabilities of the grandmother. She was seen as a strong, resourceful Afro-Caribbean woman who could take on the task of supervising her daughter's care of her granddaughter, although she had so many stresses and recent tragedies in her life that she was clearly in need of support for herself (London Borough of Lambeth, 1987).

Bearing these issues in mind, let us now turn to a systematic study of each of the four practice questions.

QUESTION 1: IS THIS A CHILD PROTECTION ISSUE NEEDING SOME RESPONSE?

One common consequence of the increased public concern about child abuse has been a steady increase in the number of referrals to child protection services in recent years. In the USA, the number of official reports has risen steadily since the 1960s. In Chapter 4, I quoted Hacking's figures of a rise from 7,000 in 1967 to 2.4 million in 1989. Since then, the numbers have continued to increase, with 3.1 million reports in 1996 (Waldfogel, 1998: 7).

A similar pattern has been identified in Canada (Johnson and Chisholm, 1989) and Australia (Parton et al., 1997: 2). In Britain, no comparable statistics have been collected but if the numbers on the child protection register are used as an indirect marker, a similar, persistent increase in the numbers of children coming to professional attention can be seen, with a tripling of numbers between 1978 and 1994 (Parton et al., 1997: 5).

It is not clear to what extent this increase is due to greater reporting, a higher incidence of abuse or a widening of the definition of what is classified as abuse (or a combination of all three factors). There is evidence that there is relatively little increase in identified cases of serious abuse (Parton et al., 1997) and a large increase in the number of referrals that are deemed to be unfounded or unsubstantiated. Besharov estimates that the number of unfounded or unsubstantiated reports in the USA is between 55 and 65 per cent of the total (Besharov, 1990: 10). In an Australian study, 50 per cent of referrals were deemed unsubstantiated (Thorpe, 1994).

What is clear is that this steep increase in referrals causes a massive increase in workload, increasing the importance of the first level of decision making about a referral relating to the level of investigation it warrants. The two main factors to consider are the *urgency* with which the child's safety needs to be ascertained and the *intensity* of the investigation. This is a very stressful stage of decision making for professionals, who know that a faulty judgement may leave a child in a dangerous situation.

Agencies and academics have devised a number of ways of classifying referrals, screening out some and prioritising those that will be investigated. In structure, these range along the analytic/intuitive continuum, at one extreme relying mainly on professional judgement and, at the other, offering an actuarial instrument for judging referrals. The Australian research reported by Parton et al. (1997) described a system relying almost exclusively on professional judgement but such professional autonomy is becoming rare. The pressure from rising numbers of referrals and from demands for equity and accountability has led most agencies to develop some guidelines on how to classify and respond to referrals, though few have been empirically tested (Wells et al., 1989).

Thorpe and Bilson (1998) offer a structured way of assessing new referrals and categorising them into matters of child *protection* or of child *concern*. The former is more serious and requires an investigation with the possibility of using coercion while the latter, which shows a lower level of concern about a child's care, is dealt with in a less adversarial atmosphere where the aim is to establish whether the parents need any support services. The criteria for classifying referrals as child protection or child concern are as follows:

Child Protection

1. An investigation is needed to further clarify information which already clearly indicates that a child has been harmed or injured, or when there is clear evidence that detailed descriptions of adult behaviours contain information about assaults on children that would normally cause harm or injury.
2. It is necessary to clarify whether actions causing harm or injury are the result of deliberate intent or are a consequence of excessive or inappropriate attempts to discipline.
3. Allegations about children arising from a number of independent sources, but with no specific reference to a harm or injury must be investigated.
4. Reports should be obtained from educational professionals, health professionals or police officers who have first-hand evidence of harm or injury to a child.

Child Concern

1. Support is required for parents having difficulty looking after their children.
2. An assessment is needed to clarify whether or not support is required.
3. Concern is expressed about the care of children but no harm or injury has been identified.
4. Information is given about the moral character of parents and concerns arise about the care of children.
5. It is necessary to identify which agency is best placed to provide a service when there is concern for the care of a child.

Training is given in any department wanting to adopt these criteria so that they are used in a consistent way.

At the analytic end of the continuum, studies have been conducted that try to identify the factors that predict which allegations will be found to be substantiated or not. To date, these attempts have had limited success though they have been superior to professional judgements (Johnson and Clancy, 1988; Wells and Anderson, 1992). Zuravin et al. (1995) reviewed existing models for prediction and found a relatively high consistency in the use of four variables:

1. *Reporter identity*: allegations from professionals were more likely to be substantiated though there was some discrepancy in which professional groups were most associated with substantiated reports.
2. *Prior reports of maltreatment*: their existence increased the likelihood of substantiation.
3. *Victim or family race/ethnicity*: there were mixed results on this. Five of nine studies found an increased likelihood of substantiation for children from ethnic minorities.
4. *Type of maltreatment*: all but one of the studies on this found that reports of physical abuse were more likely to be substantiated than those of neglect.

Zuravin et al. (1995) report a study testing a new screening instrument that achieved what the author deemed an unacceptable level of accuracy. There was a false-negative rate of 26 per cent; that is, investigators would have failed to give priority to 26 per cent; of the reports that were later found to be confirmed or indicated. The rate of false positives was 31 per cent; that is, priority would have been given to 31 per cent of allegations that were classified as ruled out or uncertain after investigation.

QUESTION 2: IS THE ALLEGATION SUBSTANTIATED AND/OR IS THERE CAUSE FOR CONCERN?

The importance of establishing what is actually going on cannot be overstated. Time and again, deaths have been shown to be due not to a failure in predicting the future but in failing to thoroughly investigate and assess the current circumstances of the child. In the case of Darryn Clarke (DHSS, 1979), for instance, repeated referrals by concerned relatives were misreported and the basic causes for their concern were not understood. Once an uncle had made a clear and impassioned statement of why he was worried about the child, professionals recognised the urgency of the matter. The three-year-old boy had recently moved with his mother to live with a man who had been violent to her in the past and had a violent criminal record. The child had twice been seen with bruises that his mother said were due to accidents and, having been a happy, cheeky, active little boy, was becoming quiet and withdrawn. Sadly, by the time the professionals had understood the referral correctly and undertaken a thorough search for the boy, he had already been fatally injured.

Investigations to follow up allegations of abuse are limited by three main factors: civil liberties, the nature of the presentation of the different forms of abuse, and resources. First, civil liberties quite rightly put limits on how much professionals can override the right to privacy of families. Relying on the co-operation of parents to establish that they are maltreating their children is obviously inadequate in most instances so every country will have criteria that establish when coercion can be used (such as when the child can be taken for a medical examination without parental consent).

A good investigation draws on evidence from other professionals in contact with the family to develop a composite account of the family (Munro, 1996), but civil liberties place limits on how much information can be shared. Many professionals have confidential relationships with the child or parents so there have to be criteria for when it is permitted to break confidentiality.

TABLE 6.2 **References on identifying abuse**

Briere J., Berliner L., Bulkley J., Jenny C. and Reid T. (eds.) (1996) *The APSAC Handbook on Child Maltreatment*. Thousand Oaks, CA: Sage.

Furnis T. (1991) *The Multi-Professional Handbook of Child Sexual Abuse*. London: Routledge.

Iwaniec D. (1995) *The Emotionally Abused and Neglected Child: Identification, Assessment and Intervention*: Chichester: John Wiley.

Meadows R. (ed.) (1997) *ABC of Child Abuse*. London, CA: BMJ.

Morgan M. (1995) *How To Interview Sexual Abuse Victims*. Thousand Oaks, CA: Sage.

Monteleone J. and Brodeur A. (eds.) (1998) *Child Maltreatment: A Clinical Guide and Reference*. St Louis, MO: G.W. Medical Publishing Inc.

Stevenson O. (1998) *Neglected Children: Issues and Dilemmas*. Oxford, Blackwell.

The importance of gaining co-operation from a family is particularly important in child protection work where the difference from a typical criminal investigation is so apparent. If police investigate a crime, the conclusion is generally a trial and a punishment for the offender. The investigating officers do not need to be worried that the offender will feel angry and hostile to them. However, if abuse is identified, in the majority of cases the plan will be to work with the parents (the offenders) and try to promote safe and adequate care in the child's birth family. Therefore, even when the law gives coercive powers, they need to be used as little and as sensitively as possible to maximise the chances of being able to work in partnership with the parents in the longer term.

The second limitation on investigations stems from the problems in identifying abuse. Each form of abuse makes substantiating allegations problematic in particular ways.

For physical abuse, the major problem is distinguishing accidental from non-accidental injuries. Medical texts provide useful summaries of the type of injuries associated, at particular ages, with abuse and accidents (Meadows, 1997; Monteleone and Brodeur, 1998). Meadows also provides a list of seven classical pointers to non-accidental injury (none are necessary or conclusive) (see Table 6.2 & Table 6.3).

Sexual abuse presents a different set of problems. The main categories of evidence are physical signs, behavioural/psychological signs, and disclosure by the victim, but they are all limited. Sometimes there are physical signs such as pregnancy or infection that prove some sexual activity has occurred but, more often, any physical signs are ambiguous. In Britain, some paediatricians thought they had found a reliable indicator of sexual abuse in the anal dilatation test but this is

TABLE 6.3 **Pointers to non-accidental injury**

1. a delay in seeking medical help (or none sought)

2. the story of the 'accident' is vague and may vary with repeated telling

3. the account is not compatible with the injury observed

4. the parents' affect is abnormal – normal parents are full of creative anxiety for their child; abusive parents tend to be more preoccupied with their own problems such as how soon they can return home

5. the parents' behaviour gives cause for concern – for example, they become hostile, rebut accusations that have not been made, and avoid seeing the consultant

6. the child's appearance and his interaction with parents are abnormal – sad, withdrawn or frightened. Full-blown 'frozen watchfulness' is a late stage; its absence does not exclude non-accidental injury

7. the child may say something. Always interview child (if old enough) in privacy. If an outpatient, child may be reluctant to open up as he is expecting to be returned to the abusing parents

now generally seen as indicative but not conclusive (Department, of Health, 1988). Even when there is strong physical evidence, investigators may then face insuperable difficulties in establishing who the perpetrator is.

Behavioural evidence also tends to be indeterminate. Many victims show no behavioural signs at the time of the abuse (Monteleone and Brodeur, 1998: 143). A number of behavioural signs reveal the possibility of abuse, the most powerful being age-inappropriate knowledge of sex. Most behavioural signs, however, are non-specific and can be seen in any child under stress: running away from home, attempting suicide, drug addiction, involvement in prostitution and juvenile delinquency.

The main source of information is disclosure by the victims. However, for a variety of reasons, many victims feel unable to talk about the abuse while it is happening and because they are still vulnerable children. They may disclose the abuse many years later as adults but they are usually then dealt with by the criminal justice system, not a child protection agency.

Research suggests that the reasons for secrecy relate to the way the abuse is conducted (Berliner and Conte, 1990). Perpetrators tend to be selective in who they target, choosing a child they have access to who is vulnerable in some way, perhaps passive, quiet, trusting, young, unhappy in appearance, needy or living in a divorced home. Once the victim is identified, the perpetrator may desensitise the child to sexual activity through a grooming process that involves a progression from non-sexual to sexual touching in the context of a gradually developing relationship. Abusers typically start with an apparently accidental touch. They also use a range of coercive tactics: separating the child from other protective adults, conditioning children through rewards and punishment, forcing children to observe violence towards their mothers, or using physical force or threatening gestures. The abuse is maintained by convincing the child it must be kept secret, making threats to harm or kill the child or someone else. When children begin to disclose the abuse, the process is often difficult and protracted and skill is needed in interviewing them (Morgan, 1995; Aldridge and Wood, 1998; Milne and Bull, 1999).

Identifying neglect and psychological abuse requires a thorough investigation that produces a comprehensive picture of the child's care over time. Unlike physical and sexual abuse, no one incident can ever provide proof. All parents are imperfect at times in their standard of care; it is the chronicity and/or the severity that justifies calling it abuse. Knowledge of child development is necessary to gauge how much the child's development and behaviour differ from the norm (Skuse, in Meadows, 1997). Knowledge of the family's culture is also crucial in making sense of their behaviour (Department of Health, 2000a). A range of evidence is needed, from interviews with the parents and child and others who know them, to direct observation of the interactions within the family and the state of the child and the home (Minty and Pattinson, 1994; Iwaniec, 1995; Stevenson, 1998). For each category of information, a number of observations are needed. Parents may be able to present a good front in one social situation but not maintain it across the board. They may be able to keep one room in the house in reasonable condition while letting other rooms fall into a state of appalling filth.

With extreme neglect, it can be hard for a professional to believe that parents could treat a child so badly. A sixteen-month-old boy died in London in 1993 having been left lying in sheets soaked in urine for several days. His body was covered in burns from the urine; he had septicaemia and septic lesions at the ends of his fingers and toes, and severe pneumonia. His parents were convicted of manslaughter but still deny any responsibility for his death (Bridge Child Care Consultancy, 1995).

A thorough assessment is needed not only to establish the existence of neglect or psychological abuse but as a base-line against which to measure change in the family. Any progress is likely to be slow and parents may resume their behaviour as soon as professional attention is reduced.

QUESTIONS 3 AND 4: DO PROFESSIONALS NEED TO INTERVENE AND HOW?

I have put these two questions together because, typically, a thorough assessment of family functioning should also identify points at which intervention could be directed.

One major issue at this stage is how comprehensive the family assessment should be. Research in both Australia (Thorpe, 1994) and England (Department of Health, 1995) has found that child protection agencies often take a narrow view of assessment, dealing only with the allegation. Yet, the families who come to their attention show many signs of stress and difficulties that will, in the long term, have a detrimental effect on the children. The English system recognises this as a problem and is trying to change and increase the number who will receive a broader assessment and services to prevent future problems. A change of policy of this nature is, however, a political decision to be made by each country.

As with screening new referrals, there has been a clear shift in practice towards more structured approaches to assessment. Practitioners will always have used some standard set of headings when making an assessment but recent models have become more structured in three ways. Many specify the issues in more detail. Some prescribe not only what is to be assessed but how it is to be measured, specifying what psychometric test or rating scale should be used to measure them, such as the Canadian 'Toronto Parenting Capacity Assessment' (Steinhauer et al., 1993). Some are more structured in specifying the theories that should inform professional thinking, as in that of the Department of Health in England (Department of Health, 2000a and b).

The case for having a more structured and less intuitive approach is very strong. While, at first glance, it might seem obvious that the more that is known about a family, the better the assessment will be, this is not necessarily so. More information may just overwhelm and confuse professionals so that they are *less* able to make sense of what they know. The problem lies within the brain. Short-term memories are only capable of holding onto seven items of information at a time (plus or minus two) (Simon, 1990). Yet reasoning in making judgements and decisions is largely determined by the contents of our short-term memories (Newell and Simon, 1972). Before information can be used, it needs to be retrieved from secondary memory and put into the short-term memory. Hence, if evidence has been collected in a haphazard way, only a little of it will be drawn on in pulling together an assessment, and the selection is likely to be random, influenced more by how vivid or recent the data are than by its relevance. In contrast, a structured approach typically not only sets out the areas to be covered but *categorises* the findings so that professionals do not deal with a disabling number of items in a long list but with a manageably small number of categories.

Stage 2: What Might Happen?

The second stage in assessing risk, having reached some conclusions about what is happening, is to move on to the future. Speculations about what might happen are linked to a time frame so that decisions can be made about the urgency with which professionals need to respond. Being clear about the particular time frame also helps to draw attention to the differences between the acute and chronic forms of abuse. Is there too much concentration upon immediate risks with the result that the longer-term dangers to the child's development are overlooked?

The clearer and more thorough the assessment of current family functioning, the easier it is to predict what might happen. Speculations fall into three main groups:

1. Will the current problematic behaviour continue?
2. What will be the impact of known imminent events on family functioning?
3. Will parental behaviour change significantly and become more dangerous?

First, there are the cases where the family might continue with much the same style of parenting unless there is professional intervention. This might pose an immediate threat to the child, such as in those cases where the parents are using extreme forms of discipline or punishment. In many cases, though, it is the longer-term impact of the continuation that causes concern. Research findings confirm that a parent who is constantly cold and critical towards a child is likely to harm that child's development of self-esteem and have many other adverse effects on the child's ability to function in adult life.

The second group is where it is known that a major change is about to occur and there is concern about what impact this will have. One classic scenario is where a family is already stressed and struggling to cope and the mother becomes pregnant. What impact will the arrival of a new baby have? Another frequent situation is where a violent partner is due to be released from prison or the mother is planning to cohabit with a man with a record of violence.

The third group is where the predictions are about new behaviour. This may be about a significant escalation of current behaviour – a pattern of increasingly harsh chastisement leading professionals to speculate that this may become even more cruel and harmful. Sometimes it is about how parents will behave in a new situation they are about to enter. How will a teenage girl with drug addiction and no supportive family behave as a mother? This group of predictions is, in many ways, the hardest to deal with and causes the most stress to professionals.

Stage 3: How Likely Are These Outcomes?

Emotions colour ideas about how probable certain events are. The tragic image of a dead child can capture the attention so strongly that it is easy to forget to look dispassionately at how likely this is to happen. One person's high anxiety about a child can sweep the rest of the team along

TABLE 6.4   **Factors for change**

1. How long has the concerning behaviour persisted?
2. In how many different contexts has it persisted?
3. What is your hypothesis about why the parent behaves in this way?
4. Does this give any indication of what factors might lead the parent to change?
5. Are any of these factors likely to occur naturally in the near future?

into an overreaction to the facts of the case. One strategy for coping with this interference is to be open about the impact the case is having on you. Discussion with a supervisor or colleague about the strong emotions generated and their impact on skewing perceptions is vitally important. If, for example, a particular case is a vivid reminder of a previous one that had a bad outcome, discuss how similar it is or whether it is one chance resemblance that is affecting your judgement.

For the most part, estimates of probability are highly speculative, but they do differ between the three clusters of predictions I described above.

If the prediction essentially relates to whether the current pattern of behaviour will continue, then there is a strong element of continuity to human behaviour. To complicate matters, though, people are always capable of change and maturation. There is a tendency in child protection work for a 'rule of optimism' to operate (Dingwall et al., 1987), for professionals to give parents the benefit of the doubt and to hope for the best. Indeed, some professionals think it is a virtue to be optimistic about human nature and can be highly critical of colleagues who express negative, and in their view, pessimistic, assessments of parents, feeling it is unfair to condemn someone for their past actions. However, kindness to the parents has to be balanced against kindness to the child, a difficult computation.

Whether growth or continuity will dominate in a particular family is hard to determine but the more thorough the assessment, the more accurately it can be done. Factors to consider can be found in Table 6.4.

With the second group of predictions, sometimes, there will be useful evidence in the family's own history of how, for instance, they coped with a new baby. In general, however, knowledge about how other people have reacted in these new circumstances has to be relied on. This set of predictions tends to be quite speculative.

The third group of predictions encompasses the families, and here it would be most helpful to be able to make accurate predictions. Which of the many dysfunctional families known to a child protection agency will deteriorate so significantly that the level of danger to their children rises sharply? As I discussed in Chapter 5, estimating the probability is difficult, especially if extreme violence and other harmful behaviour are the issues of concern. As deaths and very serious harm are statistically rare events, identifying factors that can predict them with a high degree of accuracy is hard.

Stage 4: How Undesirable Are They?

An adverse outcome may be highly probable but this, on its own, does not lead to a high-risk assessment. A judgement is also needed on how adverse it is. There may be a high chance of chronic low-level neglect but an agency might give this a lower overall assessment than another case with only a moderate probability but one of *serious* injury (or death) to the child.

Evaluating the undesirability of a risk necessarily has a subjective element. Each person's values and interests will influence that person's judgement of the relative importance of the different risks being considered. The general public seem to place a much higher value on the acute pain of a one-off physical injury than on the chronic misery of psychological abuse. Professionals, being aware of how harmful the latter is to the child's long-term well-being, might rate them very differently. This subjectivity leads to conflict. The individual professionals working on a case may disagree strongly with one another. Professional views also may conflict with those of the child victim, the family members, and the wider society.

Discussions of how seriously to rate an incident of abuse can be a disturbing process since it can feel as if some forms of abuse are being condoned through being regarded as less significant. In practice, though, judgements have to be made about where limited professional time and scarce resources should be directed.

Stage 5: The Overall Judgement of Risk – a Combination of the Likelihood and the Seriousness

Having gone through all these stages, professionals compute the different variables into an overall assessment of the degree of risk to the child. Unless an actuarial instrument has been used, this will be an intuitive judgement based on the facts, the conjectures, and the values in the case but it can be more or less explicit and structured depending on how the preceding stages have been conducted.

Few professionals will finish a risk assessment with a precise mathematical conclusion. They are more likely to use categories shaped by the thresholds for action they have to consider next. Is the risk so low that the case can be closed? Are there causes for concern in the parenting but no immediate danger? Are there imminent threats to the child's safety so that urgent intervention is needed, using coercion if the parents will not co-operate? No risk assessment should end with the crude division into safe or dangerous because this does not reflect the nature of probability assessments nor does it reflect the questions that need to be answered in practice.

The following two detailed examples illustrate how this framework can be used.

CASE EXAMPLES OF RISK ASSESSMENT

Case One

Stage 1: What Is or Has Been Happening?

The reason for referral: John, aged eight months, came to the attention of the child welfare team when his parents came to the office asking for financial help. They had just moved from a neighbouring area and said that John's name was on the child protection register there. Subsequent inquiries found that he was registered under the category of neglect. The causes for concern had been poor weight gain, inadequate clothing, and poor standards of hygiene. The family had moved suddenly, leaving substantial debts behind them. The social worker now had the task of reassessing the risk to John.

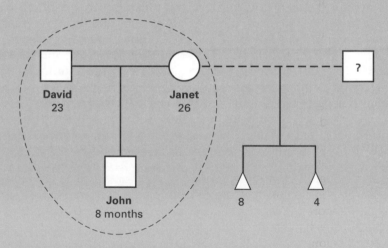

FIGURE 6.1   Case one family genogram

Background Information

Both John's parents have mild learning difficulties and have literacy and numeracy problems. Neither has ever had a job.

Janet, of white English origin, has little contact with her family. Her mother left home when Janet was nine years old and Janet took over household responsibilities for her two younger sisters. She was beaten by her birth father and raped twice by her mother's new partners. One of these was subsequently charged and convicted. She and her sisters were taken into care when Janet was fourteen. She left school at sixteen with no qualifications.

She had two children when she was aged eighteen and twenty-two by a previous partner, who was violent to her. Because of this violence and the poor level of care the children were receiving, they were removed from her, and later adopted.

David, of white English origin, was born deaf and learned to lip-read and sign. His condition was treated and his hearing was normal by age nine. His father was violent to him and his sister. He was a victim of sexual assault by a stranger when aged fourteen. He became prone to panic attacks and severe anxiety and avoided social contact. He left school at the age of sixteen with no qualifications. He has little contact with his family now.

Social circumstances: the family live on state benefits and live in a privately rented flat. They presented as socially isolated and appeared to be prey to exploitation by others.

John was a wanted and planned child. Janet attended antenatal appointments and it was a normal pregnancy and delivery. He is small with a below-average weight. He has had several sharp drops in weight associated with chest infections, colds, and stomach bugs. He appeared to have suffered from a number of illnesses but his parents did not seek medical help. He was often seen inadequately dressed and feeling cold, with swollen, red hands and feet. He appears alert and responsive to his parents, displaying appropriate anxiety when they left the room. On getting to know him better, the social worker became concerned about his seemingly indiscriminate responses. The paediatric examination revealed no concerns except about his weight, for which no organic cause could be found. The paediatrician recommended the continued monitoring of his weight.

Information for this assessment was obtained from the records of the family's previous local authority and their medical records, two meetings of professionals involved with the family, a paediatric examination, four interviews with the parents, and four observations of the child and the parent/child relationship, including observing family meals.

The parents were offered support while the assessment was going on. A social work assistant became involved to offer help in budgeting, shopping, and other practical issues the parents had identified as problematic to them.

The key concerns in the current quality of care John was receiving were as follows:

- John was failing to thrive.
- He was cold and inadequately dressed on several occasions.
- He spent long periods in his pushchair and was understimulated.
- His parents lacked adequate knowledge of his needs.

The social worker's conclusion was that John is currently suffering from neglect.

Stage 2: What Might Happen?

Short-term concerns: without intervention, the neglect might continue, harming John's early development.
Long-term concerns: without intervention, the effects of this neglect on John's development might become very serious.

Stage 3: How Likely Are These Outcomes?

Given the enduring nature of the parents' behaviour patterns to date, both the short- the and long-term consequences are very likely.

Stage 4: How Undesirable Are They?

The harmful effects on the child would be chronic and insidious rather than dramatic and acutely dangerous. To the social worker, they seemed very undesirable since they would seriously affect John's life opportunities.

Stage 5: The Overall Judgement of Risk – A Combination of the Likelihood and the Seriousness

John was suffering neglect and was highly likely to continue doing so, with increasingly severe effects on his physical and psychological development.

Case Two

This case involves a family of four children. This risk assessment relates specifically to Steven, age twelve, the second oldest child, although it necessarily includes some information about his siblings.

Stage 1: What Is or Has Been Happening?

The reason for referral: a Police Protection Order was made after all four children were found alone in the family home at 2 a.m. The house was described by a police officer as cold, with broken glass on the floor, and bare electric wires within reach. The children were returned home the following day when their mother had been helped to make the house safe and had signed an agreement not to leave the children unattended again. The family had been known to social services for many years and the children had been on the child protection register for three years, under the category of neglect and physical injury. The social worker now had the task of assessing the current risk to each of the children.

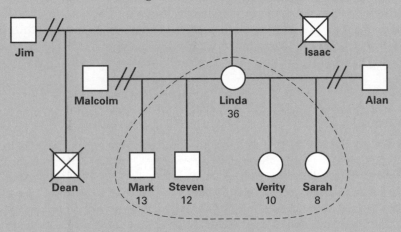

FIGURE 6.2 Case two family genogram

Background Information

The mother had been referred to social services fifteen years earlier when her first child was born. The health visitor was concerned about her lack of interest in the baby. The baby died at eleven weeks from a strangulated hernia. She had subsequently given birth to four children, with three different fathers, none of whom are currently involved with the family. She received support services from the health visitor and social services. The first significant concern about physical abuse was when Steven was seven and received cigarette burns to his wrists that a paediatrician advised were non-accidental. Steven and his family were unable to explain the injuries. He was placed on the child protection register for three months and monitored but there were no further injuries and his name was removed. No assessment was made at this time of his or his siblings' wider needs. Steven's cousin made several allegations that he had been injured by Steven's mother, Linda. These were considered true and measures were taken to protect him from further contact. Four years ago, Steven had been taken into care because his mother said she could not cope with him. He returned home after two days and Linda failed to attend appointments to discuss her problems further. Steven's name was again placed on the child protection register three years ago after he suffered facial bruising that his elder brother said were inflicted by his mother. All his siblings' names were added to the register soon after because of concerns about hygiene, supervision, stimulation, and general care. Linda refused to co-operate with an assessment or let the children be seen and it was decided there were insufficient grounds to seek legal authority to impose an assessment. The Royal Society for the Prevention of Cruelty to Animals (RSPCA) removed the family's three dogs. The mother was charged and convicted for cruelty and received a lifetime ban on keeping pets.

Current assessment: The social worker's investigation of what was currently happening found that there were a number of concerns about the children's welfare. The eldest boy, Mark, was seriously below average height and weight. He claimed that Linda had recently hit him with a stick, causing bruising to his arms and legs. Both the boys had moderate learning difficulties and attended special schools. Mark was withdrawn at school and Steven was alternately withdrawn and aggressive to his peers and adults. The older girl, Verity, would occasionally refuse to eat, saying she wanted to lose weight. The younger girl, Sarah, was estimated to be between one and two years below average in her physical and psychological development.

The social worker spent considerable time in assessing the quality of Steven's relationship with his mother and trying to ascertain his perspective. This was difficult because Steven was a generally withdrawn child who talked little. He said that he wanted to stay with his mother. She had told the children that the social services were planning to take them away and that she would kill herself if this happened. The social worker used attachment theory to provide a way of measuring the parent/child relationship, especially the degree to which it gave Steven sufficient security. The health visitor's, social work, and school records gave information about the relationship in the past, and current interactions were observed by the social worker. The records showed continuing concerns about the poor quality of attachment and the low level of stimulation and attention. Steven, at age four, had witnessed and been extremely distressed by a partner's repeated violence towards his mother. There were repeated reports of his reluctance to go home. The social worker checked the times of these reports against the presence or absence of the violent partner (the couple had several brief separations), and found he was *more willing* to go home when the partner was there. Steven went to a boarding school when he was aged ten and was keen to spend as little time at home as possible. From the total array of evidence gathered, the social worker concluded that Steven's relationship with his mother was not giving him the security and reassurance to be independent and confident. He had poor social skills and no friends. He was often aggressive to his peers. This revealed a pattern of alternating between being withdrawn and aggressive. The mother's discipline was very erratic and inconsistent.

The social worker concluded that Steven was suffering intermittent moderate physical abuse and chronic neglect.

Stage 2: What Might Happen?

In the short term: the physical abuse and neglect will continue. The physical abuse might become more serious.
In the long term: Steven already shows many signs of problems and may develop with severe difficulties in social contact and in managing his aggression.

Stage 3: How Likely Are These Outcomes?

The evidence suggests that, without intervention, the neglect due to the poor relationship with his mother is highly likely to continue. The chronicity of her difficulties makes spontaneous improvement unlikely. The mother has consistently refused to recognise there are problems in her parenting skills and has refused help from professionals. The risk of further physical abuse remains high for the same reasons. The possibility of this escalating is hard to compute but is not likely to be high.
Steven is likely to challenge his mother's authority more as he moves into adolescence, possibly precipitating a major breakdown in their relationship.

Stage 4: How Undesirable Are They?

The damage to Steven's psychological development, both in the short and long term, would be highly undesirable, as would serious physical abuse. Continuing physical abuse at the current level would be moderately undesirable.

Stage 5: The Overall Judgement of Risk – A Combination of the Likelihood and the Seriousness

Steven is at high risk of a serious level of neglect and a moderate level of physical abuse.

CONCLUSION

The best predictor of future behaviour is past behaviour. Therefore, the main task in a risk assessment is investigating and assessing what has been or is happening in the family. Any investigation is limited by civil liberties, by the amount of resources an agency can afford to put into following up an allegation of abuse, and, most importantly, by the particular problems each type of abuse presents in identification.

When a referral is made, the information is often a mixture of details about what is said to have happened, speculation about what might happen, and moral judgements on the parents' general behaviour. Separating out the facts, emotions and value judgements in a case makes it easier to deal with each stage of the risk assessment process.

Predictions of the future take three main forms: predicting that the current behaviour will continue with accumulating harm to the child; predicting the impact of known future events, such as the birth of a new baby; and predicting an escalation of current maltreatment to a serious level. In the first group of predictions, a long-established pattern of behaviour seems likely to continue, other things being equal, but human beings are capable of change and maturation, and factors outside the knowledge of professionals can alter the course of events radically. The other two groups of predictions require more substantial speculation about what new behaviour might occur. Here, professionals are considerably hampered by the low level of knowledge about human behaviour. The existing body of research on predictors of violent behaviour does not provide sufficient information to enable accurate prediction of which parents will become highly dangerous to their children.

In the best risk assessment, the responsible professionals can explain how and why they reached their final judgement. Their conclusion is defensible. It is, however, fallible and this crucial point needs to be kept in mind throughout the subsequent progress of a case. New information may cause a fundamental reappraisal of the family, whether they were deemed safe or dangerous. Professionals need to remain open to reviewing and revising their judgements.

Assessing risk should also be seen as an ongoing process. Risk assessments are done on the basis of our knowledge at one particular time so need to be continually reassessed as the child's circumstances alter. For example, the immediate risk to a child may fall dramatically if the abusive parent is sent to prison; the risk may rise if the family experiences a major event such as the birth of a new baby. The difficulties in reviewing and revising judgements are discussed in detail in Chapter 8.

The fallibility of risk assessment highlights the importance of the quality of the subsequent risk management. A system such as the British one, where the vast majority of cases are closed without offering any help, heightens the importance of the initial risk assessment because there may be no further contact and so no chance of realising that the judgement on safety was wrong. If there are support services available so that low-risk but stressed parents stay in touch with professionals, this not only reduces the chances of deterioration but also provides an ongoing opportunity to reassess them and pick up evidence that the original risk assessment was inaccurate.

SUMMARY

- The best predictor of future behaviour is past behaviour. A thorough assessment of what is or has been happening to the child is essential.
- The question 'what is happening?' is deceptively simple. It encompasses a range of questions, from a narrow focus on the alleged incident of abuse to a thorough assessment of how the family is functioning.
- Efforts to establish what is going on are hampered by three main factors: civil liberties, resources, and how the different types of abuse are presented.
- A risk assessment should refer to an explicit time frame. An emphasis on short-term dangers may undervalue the more insidious and harmful dangers the child is exposed to.
- In assessing the overall risk, a distinction needs to be made between the *likelihood* of something happening and its *undesirability*.
- Risk assessments are fallible and people's circumstances are persistently changing, so professionals need to keep their judgements under continual critical review.

7

making decisions

Decision theorists portray people as thoughtful decision makers, putting time and effort into considering alternative actions, deliberating about their possible consequences, and choosing the option that seems most likely to satisfy their goals. In contrast, the most striking feature of studies about how people actually reason is that they are revealed to be reluctant decision makers: the individual is 'beset by conflict, doubts and worry, struggling with incongruous longings, antipathies, and loyalties, and seeking relief by procrastinating, rationalizing, or denying responsibility for his own choices' (Janis and Mann, 1977: 15). Even when circumstances force people to make some decision, they fail to live up to the prescriptions of the theorists. Often the decision is made first and the thinking done later, looking for reasons to justify the choice retrospectively (Klein, 2000: 11). When people do consider a number of options, they frequently stop as soon as they come across one that seems 'good enough' (Simon, 1957), without worrying that a much better choice may be overlooked.

In child protection work, a reluctance to make decisions shows up both in avoiding decisions altogether and a tendency to procrastinate so that decisions are made in reaction to a crisis rather than as a long-term plan of how to work with a family. Children in public care have been particularly vulnerable to a failure of active decision making. Many have been left to drift, often with no clear long-term plans but a vague hope that they will eventually be reunited with their birth family (DHSS, 1985). But the same element of drift has shown up in studies of direct work with families, with practitioners being shown to be reactive, dealing with crises as they arise, but not taking a *proactive* approach to planning what work needs to be done (e.g. Farmer and Owen, 1995).

Child protection services now try to counteract this passivity by building in time scales, prescribing deadlines by which an assessment must be completed or a plan reviewed. Some states in the USA have set limits on how long children may stay in foster care before permanent arrangements are made for them. Britain has a system of fixed case reviews and a very prescriptive timetable for conducting a child abuse investigation (Department of Health, 1999).

These deadlines seem straightforwardly good practice so why has it been necessary to make them so formal? People tend to be reluctant decision makers because it is a hard task. The academics who study decision making focus on the intellectual difficulties. Many of the decisions in child protection work are, indeed, intellectually challenging and it is this dimension that receives most attention in this chapter. But decisions can also be hard because they are emotionally challenging. Making decisions that will cause distress to the people involved is painful and it is also a common feature of child protection work.

Case Example A

Amy was a two-month-old baby with leukaemia and a life expectancy of only a few months. She had been in hospital since birth but was ready for discharge. Her parents, who were heroin addicts, had two older children who had been taken permanently into care because of persistent neglect. The mother had stayed off drugs since becoming pregnant and was desperate to look after her child. However, the child's medical needs were very complex and demanding for any mother to meet. These parents had a very poor record of being able to meet the needs of healthy children. Coupled to this, providing terminal care would be an immense emotional challenge to Amy's parents, increasing the probability that the mother might return to drug misuse to help her cope. The only positive sign was that the mother had been able to stay off drugs for eight months. The workers involved with the family found it very hard to reach a decision about whether the parents should take the baby home. Intellectually, though, they did not find it difficult to reach the judgement that there was a strong probability that the baby would receive inadequate care with her birth parents. The obstacle was their sympathy for the mother, who was an appealing, dependent woman who aroused a protective instinct in many of them so that they were reluctant to give her the harsh news that she could not have sole charge of her baby as she wanted.

Decisions can also be emotionally hard because professionals know that they are only able to offer an imperfect solution and this is demoralising.

Case Example B

Dean was a fifteen-year-old who had been in care for five years after being sexually abused by his father for many years. Two years before, he had sexually abused his foster carers' eight-year-old daughter and a girl at school. He had been sent to a series of therapeutic institutions but his behaviour was so challenging and aggressive that he was to be discharged after a short time with no sign of improvement. The only option the practitioner could find for him now was a secure unit. It did not have a good reputation and, while it would provide containment, the practitioner had little hope that it would provide any effective help to Dean. His future, therefore, looked bleak and a transfer into the criminal justice system seemed a strong likelihood in the near future. Making the decision to use the secure unit was easy in that the practitioner could think of no other course of action but difficult in that it brought home the limits of her and her agency's abilities in helping such a damaged boy.

Another factor that can make decisions hard is power. Increasingly, professionals are encouraged to share power with the parents and/or the children. The arguments for this are both ethical – respecting the family's right to participate in decisions that affect them – and technical – their co-operation will increase the chance of plans being successfully implemented. To this end, working in partnership with the family is considered good practice. One consequence is that agreement can be hard to reach. Professionals may have to accept what, to them, is a sub-optimal choice because it can be assented to by all concerned. Children's participation can create particularly acute problems for professionals, who may be unsure about how mature and competent they are to make a decision. The big decisions in child protection are rarely made by one person in isolation. They usually involve both a number of professionals and family members and require a juggling act to give due weight to a range of opinions.

Given the difficulty, it seems a good idea to turn to the literature on decision making for advice on improving our skills. There are two schools of research: the decision theorists, who draw on probability theory and logic to *prescribe* a model for making decisions, and the naturalists, who aim to *describe* how people actually make decisions. Both sets of literature have useful lessons. It is untenable to claim that there is one 'right' method to be used for every decision problem. Child protection work requires decision making in a range of different contexts. For instance, an interview with a family comprises numerous microdecisions on how to proceed that have to be made swiftly and, to a large extent, intuitively, whereas a decision to remove a child from the birth family on a permanent basis is made only after considerable deliberation and needs to be explained and justified in detail both to the family and to the legal system.

Two factors that have a major influence on the way we approach a decision are how long we have to make the decision and how important it is. Practitioners in the middle of a tense interview with parents cannot sit down and start drawing decision trees to guide their choices. Nor would it be sensible, except in very exceptional circumstances, to call a meeting of several professionals and spend an hour discussing whether a child should have a dental check-up. Equally, if the decision to be made centred on whether the child should be taken away from the birth family, we would not expect professionals to make an instant, intuitive choice without due deliberation.

In this chapter, I shall be looking at the evidence on methods actually used in making decisions and considering their strengths and weaknesses in a child protection context. I shall then argue that there is a case for using formal decision theory because it offers a framework for organising reasoning and ensuring that significant details are not overlooked. There are two main areas where it offers help. The first area is when professionals are struggling to reach a conclusion and feeling confused or overwhelmed by the number of factors they are trying to consider. Decision theory helps to simplify difficult problems by breaking them down into their component parts. Second, decision theory is useful when major decisions about the welfare of a child are being made. The importance of the subject – the well-being of a child – puts a responsibility on professionals to try and make the best possible decisions. These decisions also need to be made in as clear and open a manner as possible so that others are able to understand how they were reached.

Decisions should not be judged by their outcome: fallibility is an inevitable aspect of the work. They should be judged on the way that they were reached. Professionals need to be able to demonstrate that their final choice, however well or badly it turns out in the future, was well reasoned and defensible.

SATISFICING

A common strategy for decision making was first described by Simon (1957) and labelled 'satisficing', in contrast with the 'optimizing' that is assumed by formal decision theorists. It is used when making a choice from a set of options that are met one at a time and the decision maker does not know in advance what they may be like. Simon offers the example of searching for a marriage partner. Satisficing takes the shortcut of setting an aspiration level, of what will be good enough, and stopping the search as soon as an option above this level is found. Unlike decision theory, it is not necessary to find out about all the alternatives and their consequences so there is less demand on resources.

> **Case Example C**
>
> The duty social worker was called out at 2 a.m. by the police to make arrangements for the care of two boys, aged six and eight. Their parents had been in a fight, the father had been taken to hospital and the police were about to take the mother to the police station to charge her. A crowd had collected around the house, alerted by the noise and emergency vehicles, so the worker was able to make some enquiries about relatives and neighbours. He found that the next-door neighbours, who had teenage children, knew the boys well and were willing to take them in for the remainder of the night, or even for a few nights if necessary. The worker checked that the police knew nothing worrying about this couple and accepted their offer. He did not go on searching for other possibly viable arrangements but accepted the first 'good enough' solution he found.

Simon argues that the satisficing approach is superior to formal decision theory in that it better matches the range of reasoning skills, making feasible demands on the brain's limited ability to process information. Our 'bounded rationality' leads us to resort to simplifications when faced with complex decisions: we prefer to rely on 'a drastically simplified model of the buzzing, blooming confusion that constitutes the real world' (Simon, 1957: xxix).

However, the model still presents some difficult judgements: how long should the search continue? What standard should be set? In searching for a marriage partner, people probably have little experience of past decisions to guide them. In professional practice, however, being used to making decisions in similar circumstances will help to set an achievable and good enough standard. In familiar areas of child protection, experienced practitioners probably make considerable use of this speedy method of reaching a decision. Decisions about how thoroughly to conduct an investigation, when to stop searching for more evidence, when the assessment is 'good enough' to move onto the planning stage, are all examples of the type of decisions that will draw on past experience, putting limits on the amount of thinking necessary before deciding how to act.

It is more problematic, though, when the relevant experience is lacking. Theorists have devised a number of formal ways to help work out an acceptable standard in a new subject area. However, without experience to sharpen the intuitive judgements, these quickly become complex and time-consuming so that satisficing loses its merit as a swift way to reach a decision (Gigernzer et al., 1999: 14).

Ignorance of appropriate standards may not just be because the professional is a novice but because the nature of the decision makes it hard to acquire knowledge of the long-term outcomes. The way child protection services are organised can prevent professionals from building up background knowledge. A duty team that is only involved on a short-term basis can make organisational sense but, in terms of developing practice wisdom, is not able to provide long-term evidence of the consequences of the choices made by the staff.

The long-term results of decisions can often be ascertained only by empirical research. The outcomes for children in public care, for example, can be determined only by large-scale studies. The individual does not have the length or range of experience to build up a reliable picture of how children will cope. But, sadly, research on public care highlights a feature often found in child protection work; outcomes are poor. Despite some cases of extremely happy results, most children who spend lengthy periods in public care experience significant difficulties as adults (Thoburn, 1990). With this background knowledge, professionals are not looking for a placement that is 'good enough' but the 'best possible' since, with such an intractable problem, even this is likely to be inadequate. In practice, it often feels to professionals as if they are looking for the 'least bad' option for the child, knowing as they do the problems both of staying with an abusive birth family and of making secure relationships in a new family.

PATTERN RECOGNITION DECISION MAKING

Klein's (2000) research studied professional people making important decisions under pressure of time. He spent time with firefighters, for example, accompanying them to fires, watching them make split-second decisions on how to tackle the blaze, and later discussing how they made their choices on what to do. He concluded that expert firefighters were not using formal analytic methods of reasoning but the power of intuition, mental simulation, metaphor, and storytelling.

> The power of intuition enables us to size up a situation quickly. The power of mental simulation lets us imagine how a course of action might be carried out. The power of metaphor lets us draw on our experience by suggesting parallels between the current situations and something else we have come across. The power of storytelling helps us consolidate our experiences to make them available in the future, either to ourselves or to others. (Klein, 2000: 3)

The 'recognition-primed decision model' proposed by Klein has two components: the way decision makers size up the situation to recognise which course of action makes sense, and the way they evaluate that course of action by imagining it. An experienced decision maker will be able to recognise patterns, to see similarities between the current problem and past problems that have been worked through to a solution. This helps them set priorities about what needs to be tackled first, to know what information is essential, and gives them an idea of what to expect next. By recognising a situation as typical, they also recognise a course of action likely to succeed. They do not just act on their decision uncritically but continue to evaluate it as they implement it by using their imagination. This enables them to check their assessment against the past and the future. They weave a story around the known features of the situation to see whether they can all plausibly be fitted into the scenario they have recognised. They also use their imagination to project into the future. They mentally simulate what should happen if their story is correct so that they can prepare for it and, if the unexpected happens, it makes them question its accuracy.

> A firefighting team respond to a report of a basement fire in a four-story build-
> ing. The commander arrives quickly and does not see anything from the out-
> side. There are no signs of smoke anywhere. He enters via the door to the
> basement and sees flames spreading up the laundry chute. He recognises a ver-
> tical fire that will spread straight up and knows how to deal with it. Since there
> are no external signs of smoke, it must just be starting. But fire crews sent up to
> spray water down the chute report that it has gone beyond the second floor. It
> cannot, therefore, have just started and his assessment was wrong. He goes out-
> side and now sees smoke emerging from the eaves of the roof. He recognises a
> new pattern: the fire started some time ago and spread directly up the chute so
> that no smoke escaped. This leads to a completely new decision on how to
> respond. Putting the fire out is no longer the priority. The first action must be to
> evacuate the building and so he instigates a search and rescue operation.
> (adapted from Klein, 2000: 15)

After he had recognised the problem as a vertical fire, experience of similar fires meant that the commander had a complete story in his mind of how it should have started and how it would behave. He could, there-fore, make a swift decision on how to respond and an equally swift reappraisal when he recognised that new information did not fit the story.

I shall be discussing the evaluative methods in this model of decision making in more detail in the following chapter but, at this point, the features I want to concentrate on are its emphasis on experience and imagination. This seems to fit with the way many child protection work-ers would say they are operating much of the time. The duty worker, tak-ing a new referral, makes a swift appraisal of whether there is anything in the information that requires an instant response. This is not usually based just on the specific content of the referral. It might take into account who is making the allegation, what else is known about them, and how reliable they seem as informants. It might also consider what is known about the family in question. An apparently minor allegation relating to a family about whom there is already a high degree of concern might ring alarm bells and prompt an urgent reaction. The decision maker also has to take account of the agency's resources at that point and what it is feasible for them to do. An experienced duty officer becomes proficient in recognising what type of referral has been made and this classification provides a pattern for responding to it.

The swift intuitive appraisal is also strongly apparent in therapeutic work. Experienced family therapists, for instance, develop a set of categories of family types that enables them to size up a new family and reach decisions about how to respond to them. This typology may be more or less informed by formal theories of family dynamics but at the point at which it is used in a family interview it is being used at an intuitive level.

Where speed is crucial, this pattern-recognition model seems to have considerable relevance to child protection work. However, this model differs from formal decision theory in *not* encouraging people to think widely. The professionals making decisions under time pressure did not appear to Klein to spend much time *comparing* alternatives though this is seen as the central task in decision theory. Rather, they were *recognising* the type of decision they were dealing with and checking whether this assumption was justified. This model of decision making does not look so suitable when dealing with the major, influential decisions in child protection where there is time to think. A constant criticism made by formal theorists is that natural decision makers tend to suffer from tunnel vision.

Case Example D

When workers were deciding on the fate of Jane, a six-month-old baby who had been in care for two months after suffering a fractured arm at home, they weighed up the risks and advantages of her staying in her current foster home and of returning to her parents. They decided that there were serious concerns about the foster carers and so decided that, on balance, it would be better for Jane to return to her parents. Her father killed her two weeks later.

The problem here was that the child protection team framed the decision in terms of two options only – staying in an unsatisfactory foster home or returning to abusive parents – and, in this context, the birth family seemed the better choice. But they forgot to think about other placement options and so chose what seemed the lesser evil when there were, in fact, several better choices available.

This (true) story may be thought just to illustrate bad practice but the reality is that professionals frequently get caught up in a narrow picture of the child's circumstances. The problem of tunnel vision is a variation of the problem that some information comes to mind much more readily. As will be discussed in more detail in the next chapter, information that is recent, vivid, or emotional is more easily thought of. In this case, the professionals were confronted with two highly emotional options. The birth parents were pressing them hard to let the child go home and were making the most of a slight medical disagreement about whether the injury could have actually been accidental as the parents claimed. At the same time, the foster carers were wanting to keep Jane but the social worker visiting them was getting increasingly worried about their attitude and was beginning to suspect that they were nursing a long-term hope of adopting her. So the experience was of two couples putting the workers under emotional pressure by claiming that the child would be better off with them. It is not so surprising that they fell into the trap of sharing the couples' view that the decision centred solely on which of them should have Jane.

Tunnel vision can also arise when professionals get into the habit of treating all cases with a fixed pattern of response. Klein's (2000) research showed this to be a common feature of practice and, to some extent, it is reasonable. Experienced people get to know what choices they have and do not have to approach each referral as a novice would, making time-consuming investigations to find out what alternatives are available. From time to time, however, they need to step back and think more broadly. Otherwise, there is a danger that they will fail to notice when new options are developed – perhaps a new support service becomes available. They may also not notice when the families they are dealing with change. Services that suit a mainly white British population may be less appropriate if a large group of a particular ethnic minority move into the area.

The value ascribed to thinking of a range of options is a major conflict between the formal decision theorists and those studying natural methods. There is, I believe, no absolute answer. It varies between contexts depending on two competing factors: the importance of speed in reaching a conclusion and the importance of demonstrating to others that the best possible decision has been made. At different stages in the process, child protection workers need both types of decision-making skill.

ONE-REASON DECISION MAKING

Another speedy method of making a choice is to base a decision on one reason only. This saves on the effort of trying to list several reasons and finding a way of comparing their value. In the context of finding an emergency placement for children in the middle of the night, the practitioner might base the decision on the fact that he or she had observed the children running to the neighbours for comfort. In the traumatic circumstances, this might seem sufficient evidence for thinking they could provide adequate care.

Formal models of decision making always assume that there is a common currency for beliefs and wishes; some way in which their relative value can be compared. However, this does not seem to fit all human decisions. Sometimes, one motive is so strong, it does not make sense to compare it with others. The desire to have children can be this overwhelming. Economists frequently produce statistics on the cost of bringing up a child and the impact it has, in particular, on the earning power of the mother. To a person without parental yearnings, it can look quite irrational to choose to take on such an expensive and risky enterprise. But the mother nursing her longed-for baby does not try to justify the expense; it literally does not make sense to her to compare money in the bank with the joy she is experiencing.

Ethical and legal reasons can be powerful enough to provide sufficient grounds on their own for reaching a decision. In child protection, sometimes there is a clear legal duty that rules out any alternative response. If practitioners are faced with children whose lives are in immediate danger from parents, they do not waste time considering whether to leave them in danger but act to save their lives.

One-reason decisions are defensible in some specialised contexts in child protection but, on the whole, if this method is used it is because the professional involved has not put in the effort of thinking more comprehensively.

SHORT-SIGHTED DECISION MAKING

Those who have taken over a child protection case from other workers will have had the experience of thinking that their predecessors' decisions have made life harder for them. Sometimes, this is inevitable; good decisions do not guarantee good outcomes. Sometimes, though, it is quite reasonable to consider that colleagues acted without thinking whether the action that solved a problem for them was likely to create more problems for future workers. Short-term solutions can, in practice, be time bombs, setting up a scenario that is more complex than the original.

People tend to take a short-sighted view of a problem (Keller and Ho, 1988; Fischoff, 1996). While, on one level, it is understandable that people working under pressure tend to concentrate on dealing with the immediate difficulty, it is still problematic since, in child protection work, professionals are so often involved in long-term work with a child and/or family. Failing to think about the consequences of a decision for future work with a family is poor practice.

One particular weakness of being myopic is that contingency plans are not made, plans of what to do if the more optimistic prediction is wrong and the course of action chosen cannot be pursued. This means that, in practice, a team of experienced professionals may have spent considerable time in discussing a case and setting out a plan of action but then an inexperienced front-line worker is left to make emergency plans when circumstances alter and the original plan becomes obsolete. In child protection, professionals know that they are rarely dealing with certainties and, so, they should accept that even the best-laid plans can go wrong and this should be allowed for in planning.

DECISION THEORY

Having looked at evidence on natural decision making, I now want to turn to the prescriptive model of decision theory. It sets out a framework for thinking about the possible options there are, considering what consequences there might be and how probable they are, judging how good or bad these outcomes would be, and finally picking the option that best reflects the decision maker's values and beliefs, that is, the one most likely to have the most beneficial consequences. So in terms of a child at risk, the best outcome would be that the child is uninjured and grows up to be a healthy and fairly happy adult. For most children, the best outcome is likely to result from leaving the child with his or her birth family. But in a particular case, it may be thought that, despite the benefits of being with the birth parents, this option carries a substantial risk of the child's being killed or seriously injured (and not achieving a happy adulthood). Therefore, an option such as a good foster placement is chosen, where there is a moderate probability of some undesirable consequences but very low probability of a really bad outcome. For this particular child, the foster placement has the *highest expected utility value*.

Decision Trees

A decision tree is a very effective way of organising reasoning and analysing the problem. Its clear identification of the sequence of events and the links between them in itself makes problematic decisions much easier to understand and manage. By making estimates of the likelihood and the desirability of consequences explicit in terms of numbers, it is possible to work out which option has the highest utility value, and show the grounds for the final choice. I shall gradually build up a decision tree as I go through the stages of decision making, but here are some initial comments on how to draw them:

1. In a tree, time goes from left to right.
2. There are three main types of node. A *decision* is represented by a square. A *chance* node (a consequence that is beyond the decision maker's control) is represented by a circle, and a *terminal* node, a final outcome (from the point of view of one's current interests), is shown by a triangle.
3. A tree may extend over several consequences and subsequent decision points.

TABLE 7.1   A framework for making decisions

1.   What decision is to be made?
2.   What options are there?
3.   What information is needed to help make the choice?
4.   What are the likely/possible consequences of each option?
5.   How probable is each consequence?
6.   What are the pros and cons of each consequence
      (i.e. what is their expected utility)?
7.   The final decision.

A 'rational' decision, according to decision theorists, is the one that is consistent with one's preferences about possible outcomes and one's estimates of how probable each outcome is.

Earlier, I criticised decision makers who had tunnel vision or short-sightedness. Decision theory can be just as problematic but for the opposite reason. The reasoning of informal decision makers can resemble the decision tree in Figure 7.1 but decision theory can rapidly produce a decision tree as overwhelming and complicated as Figure 7.2.

By encouraging the thinker to consider all the options and their consequences, decision theory can create a disabling number of data. When considering whether to return an abused child to his or her parents, professionals could spend weeks thinking of all the alternatives to going home, such as a range of placements or various ways of maintaining contact with the birth family. They would then have to research their feasibility before appraising all the branches of the tree. The size of the task would mean that they would be unable to reach a decision in the time frame necessary for the child's welfare. Judgement has to be exercised in deciding how much effort to put into any specific decision. Experience often helps to reduce the detail with which the framework need be applied.

Hammond et al. (1999) recommend that people should focus on the stages of the decision framework that are most problematic in a particular decision. If they begin by scanning quickly through the whole process to gain a broad perspective on the problem, they can usually identify some elements as the most crucial or difficult for that particular decision. In the case examples below, the professionals were able to do this and the framework helped them spot the points where the difficulties or controversies arose so that their intellectual efforts were targeted on these, and were not evenly spread. As a decision is analysed, it often becomes clear what should be done so that it is not necessary to follow through the whole process systematically.

Although decision theory offers a framework for making every step of the reasoning clear and public, it is important not to exaggerate its objectivity. A fully completed tree ends up as a mathematics problem, multiplying probabilities and utility values to compute the overall utility value

Decision tree

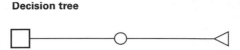

FIGURE 7.1   A simple tree

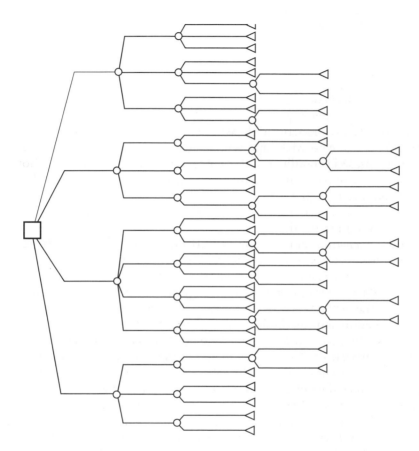

FIGURE 7.2   A complex tree

of an option. Numbers can have a powerful impact on people, giving the appearance of reliability and impartiality, but it must be remembered where the numbers came from. Constructing a decision tree requires both formal and intuitive knowledge. Listing the available options is a creative process, using imagination and practice wisdom. Deciding on the probability of each outcome is, in child protection work, largely an intuitive guess, albeit informed by empirical research to some degree. Determining the utility values of each outcome is undoubtedly a subjective process with no objectively 'right' value that everyone should agree on. Using decision theory helps to push the decision making along the analytic/intuitive continuum towards being more analytic. Analysing decisions in this way enables people to break a complicated decision process down into smaller and simpler parts. It helps but does not replace the human decision maker.

Stage 1: What Decision Is To Be Made?

☐

FIGURE 7.3 **The decision**

The first task is to determine what decision is being dealt with, how quickly it has to be made, and who needs to be involved. The way a decision is phrased can influence the subsequent reasoning, leading thoughts in one particular direction so that some relevant options are overlooked.

When a child protection service develops increasingly specific procedures and guidelines, practitioners may start to phrase questions in terms of the procedures rather than the child. 'Should we call a case conference?' 'Should this child be put on the Child Protection Register?' This guides their thoughts towards agency and case management issues and to routine ways of responding to families. If the same decision were phrased in child-focused terms, it would have a different impact. If instead of asking whether to hold a case conference, the question was, 'Do we need to investigate further to check if this child is safe?' professionals' thoughts would be directed to factors relating to this one child. What is already known about her? Does it need to be amplified or verified? What significant gaps are there in the investigation so far? Holding a case conference then becomes one of several ways of meeting the identified needs, but if one should be held, there would be a more specific agenda.

Professionals can, inadvertently, miss out a stage in the sequence of decisions in a case by framing a decision in a way that tacitly assumes some past decision has already been made. The question 'What suitable placement is there for this child?' presupposes that the decision has already been made to remove him or her. On a remote island in Scotland, in 1991, nine children were removed from their parents because of allegations of organised sexual abuse. The logistics of such a large operation in a small community were complex and, as the subsequent public inquiry reported, it appears that the police and social workers devoted much time and effort to deciding *how* to arrange the removal and where to take the children. It is not clear, however, that anyone, at any stage, gave much thought to *whether* they should be removed. The idea seems to have been conceived in the minds of the two senior managers and

> The idea, once lighted upon, remained without serious review or reappraisal. Although it cannot properly be said that … a decision had been reached by [the

senior managers] both their minds were set upon the one course which had immediately occurred to each of them. (Scottish Office, 1992: 39)

Thereafter, the decision was framed in terms of how, not whether, to take the children from their parents.

In the case example I used in talking of tunnel vision, the birth family and the foster family presented child protection staff with the task of choosing between them. Staff went along with this way of framing the decision, with disastrous consequences.

Dealing with a case of child abuse involves a series of decisions, some small and some large. They are interconnected so that a choice made at one point limits what options there are later. The assessment stage involves numerous decisions about what information to collect and how to find it. Getting to the point of making a major management decision about a case itself requires a decision. This may be a decision for the individual but, increasingly, agencies are specifying timetables for dealing with a case, and prescribing the major decision points.

Professionals benefit from experience. Experts are able to frame a situation rapidly, using their store of experience to make sense of a particular case, recognising meaningful patterns of events or actions. They can be more flexible and adaptable than novices, who are limited to surface features of the situation and, so, are more likely to do things by the book, following procedures or guidelines conscientiously (Beach, 1997). Therefore, experience helps in forming an overview of a case and judging what particular decisions have to be made at what point. The novice may feel much closer to the portrait in Chapter 1 of a decision maker steering a small boat on a stormy sea, just trying to survive the next wave.

Stage 2: What Options Are There?

After identification of what decision is being made, the second task in any decision problem is to draw up a list of the possible actions that are available.

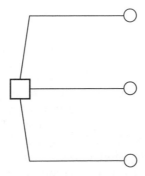

FIGURE 7.4 **The options**

The emphasis on thinking about options differentiates a decision theory approach from informal methods of decision making. As I mentioned at the beginning, people often do not consider alternatives at all but alight on one course of action and look for reasons to justify it. Even when they do consider more than one path, they reduce the effort required by giving up as soon as they reach a path that 'satisfices' their goals. Recent research in England found that in case conferences where the child was judged to be at significant risk of abuse, professionals spent most of the meeting talking about the level of risk and, on average, only nine minutes on deciding how to manage it (Farmer and Owen, 1995). Therefore, this stage in the decision process needs to be deliberately planned, to reduce the chances of professionals cutting corners.

Why should we put time and effort into thinking about options? The strongest argument is a moral one: we should be trying to find the best solution for a child. A 'good enough' one may be all we can finally obtain but our goals should be higher. A second argument is practical: we tend to be carried along by the current flow of how a case is perceived and how cases of that type are routinely dealt with by our agency. Innovation and change are only possible if we stand back and deliberately use our imagination and intelligence to think of new ways of responding to the family.

Since it is easy to become overwhelmed by a vast list of options, some should be considered and rejected as unworkable at this stage so that only a manageably small number are further investigated. Again, it is a situation where the experienced worker has advantages over the novice since the former will have more understanding of what is or is not feasible and can more rapidly dismiss some options. The ignorance of novices can sometimes, however, be an advantage. They will not be constrained by the way this type of case has always been dealt with before but may produce truly novel and valuable ideas of what might be done now.

Time constraints mean that, at the individual case level, some degree of routinisation is inevitable but it can be a useful exercise for an agency or team to set time aside occasionally for a group brainstorm about the range of options they are using with particular groups of families and whether these are adequate.

Stage 3: What Information Is Needed To Help Make the Choice?

Knowledge is obviously a crucial component of good decision making but, as was the case with thinking of too many options, we can have too much knowledge and be disabled by it. Research on decision making by social workers has supported this point (Rosen, 1981; Wells, 1988). Lewis's (1994) study of probation officers found that increasing the information available led to worse decision making. Officers provided with only a summary of the key points of the case made better decisions than those who had read the whole file. As was previously discussed in relation to gathering material for a family assessment, information needs to be

organised so that it is easily comprehensible. Decision theory provides a
framework in which this can be done.

Each stage in the decision-making process triggers a search for some
information. Indeed, the most important point for data collection is at the
earliest assessment stage. A good decision rests on the assessments of
the risks and needs of the child and the strengths and weaknesses of the
parents. The quality of the assessment strongly affects the quality of the
subsequent decisions. But I have put the question about information at
this point in my decision framework for two reasons. The compiled list of
options is the second major trigger for collecting more information, finding out more about the options that have been thought of so that it can be
judged how suitable they might be for this case. Also, since the decision
maker has now created a rough outline of the decision problem, it is
possible to collect new information systematically and file it in the relevant place in the outline. If a specific option has been listed, then what
extra knowledge is needed to decide whether it is feasible and desirable?

Stage 4: What Are the Likely/Possible Consequences of Each Option?

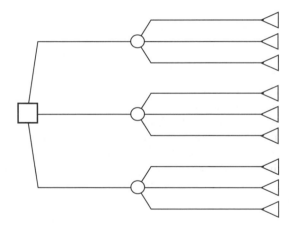

FIGURE 7.5 **The consequences**

Decision theory counteracts the natural tendency to short-sightedness by
encouraging people to think further into the future and imagine what the
consequences of the possible options might be. For instance, if deciding
what alternative care to provide for a child, the options might be finding
a foster home, a placement in a residential setting, a placement in a therapeutic setting, or placement with a relative. But for each of these options,
there is a set of possible consequences. In any one, it is possible that the
child will settle well and flourish, that the arrangement will be less than
satisfactory but will survive, or that things will be so bad that there will be
a total breakdown and new arrangements will need to be made. To generate

ideas about consequences, it is a good strategy to imagine that one particular option has been chosen and then envisage what might happen, whether it will work out well or badly.

At this stage, we are only concerned with thinking about what *could* happen, not how likely it is. Intuitively, professionals tend to hope for the best; they assume, for instance, that a satisfactory foster home will be found. However, research has shown that there is a high rate of placement breakdown so the possibility of its happening in this case should be considered. By looking further into the future, professionals are also encouraged to think about making contingency plans and identifying when they need to be activated. A conference may confidently decide to send a child to a therapeutic placement but the responsible worker may later discover that no funding is available or, after meeting each other, that either the child or the placement staff do not want to proceed with the arrangement. A back-up plan should have been made for dealing with this contingency.

Stage 5: How Probable Is Each Consequence?

If full information were available, life would be a lot easier but decisions are always made with some degree of uncertainty about what will happen if one path is followed. If a child is left with abusive parents who are offered support services, what is the probability that the parents will engage with these services, how likely are they to make progress, and what are the chances that the child will suffer further abuse?

Research, practice experience, and knowledge of a particular family and the local resources are the main sources of wisdom to help to estimate probabilities. Empirical research is useful but imperfect. Its findings are in terms of generalisations so there is considerable margin of error in extrapolating down to a particular family. Despite this, when relevant studies are available, they provide the most reliable, because most broadly based, data. Professional experience of dealing with similar families is often the only source available and this carries the risk of being a skewed sample with biased follow-up. But knowledge of the family themselves offers crucial specific information. If the probability of a satisfactory placement for a ten-year-old boy is being considered, research may report a particular level of placement breakdowns for this category. For instance, the practitioner's experience with the local fostering service may suggest that they have particular difficulty in meeting the needs of young boys. The characteristics of the boy himself will also influence the estimation. Does he exhibit particularly problematic behaviour? Is there a relevant history of previous placements? How has he fared in them?

When I have asked students to speculate about probabilities, some have found it difficult not so much at a cognitive level as at an emotional one. Some seem to fear making self-fulfilling prophecies: if we predict a poor outcome, we might cause it to happen. Some are also clearly reluctant to use evidence of a parent's past failure to predict future failure. There is a belief that we should give them the benefit of the doubt; we should not condemn them for past misconduct. We certainly should hold onto the belief that people are, to some degree, capable of solving problems and improving. However, if a father has tried to deal with an alcohol problem six times in the past, and each time been unsuccessful, then it is clearly irrational to base a plan for protecting the child on a high estimation of the likelihood of the father's success this time. This does not necessarily mean that we would prevent him from trying but we would have to have plans to deal with either success or failure.

Talking about probabilities is a part of everyday practice but where decision theory differs is in recommending the language of numbers in discussing them. Professionals tend to use qualitative language. Success for one option might be 'highly likely', 'more likely than not' or 'barely possible'. The trouble with this is that one person's 'very likely' may be someone else's 'absolutely certain'. Using numbers reduces the chance of miscommunication and sharpens thinking. In probability theory, chances are rated between 0 and 1. Something that is impossible is 0; it has no chance of happening. Something certain is rated as 1. An event which has a fifty/fifty chance is 0.5. If you have said something is 'very likely', you have to decide more precisely what you mean. Is it 0.8 likely or even higher at 0.9? These numbers can also be expressed in terms of percentages. An event that is certain has a 100 percent chance of occurring. A therapy with a 0.4 success rate means that 40 per cent of people who receive it will benefit.

If you are having trouble in specifying a number, home in from the extremes. Do you think this child will definitely settle well in his next placement? If not, how many problems do you think there might be? Would you at least think it is more likely than not?

Using numbers brings to the fore another aspect of reasoning about probabilities. The possible consequences of a particular option that have been listed at Stage 4 should cover all eventualities. Sometimes there are only a small number of clearly defined possibilities. An abusive father facing court proceedings in England will be found either guilty or not guilty. Often in child protection, however, there are numerous slightly different possible outcomes. The outcomes of a foster placement, for instance, can range from brilliant to total breakdown. To simplify matters in these cases, it can be helpful to cluster the outcomes into a small number of two or three categories ranging from 'highly satisfactory', via 'adequate but problematic' to 'failed'.

Since the set of consequences describe all that could possibly happen, their probabilities should total 1; one of them must occur. In the case of the abusive father in court, if it is thought that he is likely to be found not guilty and the probability is rated at 0.7, then, logically, the chance of his being found guilty must be 0.3. Either one or the other must happen so the sum of their probabilities must total 1.

Stage 6: What Are the Pros and Cons of Each Consequence
(i.e. What Is Their Expected Utility Value)?

Leaving a child at home has the potentially desirable consequence of
maintaining the best context for a happy upbringing, as well as the very
undesirable ones that the child may be killed or seriously injured or
suffer long-term psychological harm from the parents. The value given to
an outcome is called its *utility value*.

This stage involves value judgements and there may well be serious
differences between different people or different professions about the
utility value of particular outcomes. The general public, for instance,
tends to have rather optimistic views about foster care whereas professionals are more aware of the hidden costs in terms of loss of contact with
birth family and community. There may be significant differences
between the family and the professionals about the desirability of different outcomes. A police officer may place a high value on the successful
conviction of a sex abuser but the abuser's daughter, who was the victim,
may have very different views. To her, keeping the family intact might
have the highest value, even if this carries a risk of further abuse to her.
These are serious questions of values to which there are no right answers.

This stage in decision theory again asks professionals to move from
qualitative to quantitative language. Outcomes are evaluated in practice
and some are clearly preferred to others, but these judgements tend to be
expressed in often emotive words. The death of children from abuse is
'terrible'; their satisfactory rehabilitation is 'great'. Asking people to put a
number on the desirability of an outcome encourages them to think about
the many factors that are implicitly influencing their judgements. The
clear instruction to think about the pros, as well as the cons, helps to counteract any optimistic or pessimistic bias. This can be particularly useful in
child protection if the agency is tending towards a very defensive style of
practice. The exercise, when done as a group, can also bring out the
different values and priorities of the different professionals involved.
Senior managers, for example, tend to put far greater weight on the
financial costs of an outcome than do front-line workers.

The following exercise to determine utility values in a hypothetical case
does not need to be repeated with every decision. Practitioners build up a
set of preferences over time and apply them intuitively to a new case. It
can, however, be helpful for an agency or team to undertake this exercise
from time to time in relation to particular groups of cases to clarify their
thinking and find out what variations there are within the work group in
how they evaluate outcomes. It may not resolve all disputes (and some
degree of difference is to be expected) but it does help people with
extremely different values to understand why they disagree with their colleagues. The exercise also serves to illustrate the constant tension in child
protection between protecting a child and preserving a family. If keeping a
child alive were the only objective of a child protection system, evaluating
outcomes would be relatively simple. Professionals, however, are also

TABLE 7.2   Exercise in assigning utility

Consequence	Pros	Cons	Utility value

working to the objective of maximising the child's welfare and the birth family, in most cases, has a lot to offer in achieving this goal.

The chart in Table 7.2 provides columns for listing the pros and cons of a possible consequence of a particular option. In completing it, you might consider factors relating to the welfare of the child, his or her siblings and parents, the impact on the professionals, the cost to the agency or to society, and the effect on society or on other clients. In the final column, you put the utility value between 0 (very undesirable) and 10 (highly desirable) as an overall measure of that consequence, taking into consideration both its good and bad features. If a consequence seems evenly balanced between good and bad effects, you would rate it midway at 5. An appalling consequence might be rated at 0. The values you assign should express your preferences. If you think consequence X is better than Y, then you should give it a higher value. The value you choose is a subjective judgement, reflecting your knowledge, values and preferences. It is not right or wrong in any absolute sense. People vary greatly in their tolerance of adverse outcomes. For some, negative consequences weigh very heavily and for others it is the reverse. In child protection, the options we face often compel us to compare the value on maximising the child's welfare while minimising any risk of harm. An agency that has suffered the tragic death of a child may react by becoming very defensive and, wanting to minimise the possibility of another death, place less value on the consequences that promote the child's welfare in other respects. The basic principle in assigning utility values is that 'the more desirable the better consequences of a risk profile relative to the poorer consequences, the more willing you will be to take the risks necessary to get there' (Hammond et al., 1999: 138).

When I have asked student groups to do this exercise, there has been some slight variation in the precise number they assign an outcome but, so far, no significant difference in the order of their preferences. The completed chart in Table 7.3 gives an example of one set of students' ratings of the consequences in a particular case where the options had been reduced to two: whether to return an abused child to the birth family or move the child to a long-term foster placement. (There has since been a significant change of policy in Britain, so that, now, adoption would more likely be considered as the alternative to rehabilitation. Also, in the option of returning to the birth family, there was a range of ideas about what supportive help they might be given, but the decision has been reduced to the two main options for the sake of simplicity.) The consequences of each option were clustered into three categories.

TABLE 7.3 **Utility assessment**

Consequence	Pros	Cons	Utility value
Rehabilitation and good care.	Birth family still united. Professional reward of seeing a success. No stigmatisation of child. Culture maintained.	Cost of monitoring and any support services provided.	9
Rehabilitation, moderate care, and continuing concerns about abuse.	Birth family still united. No stigmatisation of child. Culture maintained.	Distress to child of continuing abuse. High cost of continuing professional contact. Emotional cost to professionals of concern about child's safety.	4
Rehabilitation and serious injury/death.	Birth family still united. Less expensive than foster care. No stigmatisation of child. Culture maintained.	Pain of abuse to child. Emotional cost to parents, siblings, and professionals. Career cost to professionals of being involved in a tragedy. High cost of continuing professional contact.	0
Foster placement and good care.	Child at less of risk of abuse than at home. Basic needs met.	Disruption of family bonds. Child's feeling of loss. Continuing cost to society.	7
Foster placement and continuing problems.	Child at less of risk of abuse than at home. Basic needs met.	Disruption of family bonds. Child's feeling of loss. Damage to child's development. Continuing cost to society.	3
Foster placement breakdown.	Child at less risk of abuse than at home.	Disruption of family bonds. Child's feeling of loss both of birth family and placement. Damage to child's development. Damage to child's mental well-being from failing in a relationship. Extra cost to society of finding new placement.	1.5

The utility values reflect a belief that the birth family, other things being equal, is always a more valuable option than foster care, which has the cost not only of disrupting family relationships, but also of a constant charge on the public purse.

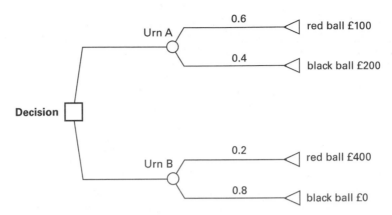

FIGURE 7.6 **Choosing urn A or B**

Stage 7: The Final Decision

Finally, after going through these stages, we choose the option whose consequences combine realistic likelihood and best desirability, producing the highest expected utility. One option might have a small risk of a fairly undesirable outcome and a good chance of a desirable result so it is preferable to another option that has a high risk of a very undesirable result even though it has a moderate chance of leading to a satisfactory conclusion.

Decision trees are a way of showing this process in a diagram. For example, suppose the choice is to pick a ball, which may be red or black, out of one of two urns, A and B (Figure 7.6). If urn A is chosen, then a red ball gains the prize of £100, and a black ball £200. It is known that three-fifths of the balls in this urn are red. In urn B, getting a red ball will win a higher prize of £400, but a black ball wins nothing. In this urn, only a fifth of the balls are red. Out of which urn will you pick a ball?

To work out the expected utility value of choosing a particular urn, you multiply each possible cash outcome by its probability and then add together all the results. So, if you have chosen urn A, in which three-fifths (60 per cent) of the balls are red, the 0.6 probability of getting a £100 prize comes to £60; the 0.4 probability of winning £200 produces £80. Add them together and the expected utility value of deciding on urn A is £140.

In urn B where only one-fifth (20 per cent) of the balls are red, there is a 0.2 probability of winning £400, which produces £80, plus an 0.8 chance of winning nothing, yielding £0, making a total expected utility value of £80. This is much less than urn A, so deciding on urn A looks a better bet.

Here are some examples of how using this decision theory approach looks in child protection scenarios. For brevity, the details in each case have been reduced to the most significant. They are based on real cases presented by my students and the probabilities and utility values are those assigned by the students.

CASE EXAMPLES

Case One

Stage 1: What Decision Is To Be Made?

Nat, age fifteen, has been in a secure unit for four weeks because he has a history of placing himself in danger during periods of absconding from home and living on the streets. It is a requirement of the legislation under which he is held that detention should be for the shortest appropriate time. The decision now has to be made whether he should be moved to an alternative placement. Nat's participation in the decision-making is required by law and his co-operation is needed if any plans are to be successfully carried out. His parents' participation is recommended by legislation but, in this case, there are significant differences between the parents and the professionals in the definition of Nat's problems so the parents' involvement is problematic.

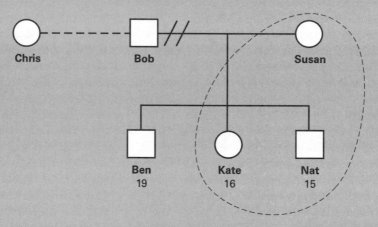

FIGURE 7.7   Case one family genogram

There is little information available about Nat's earlier childhood but there are several causes for concern. He has a history of substance abuse and offending, he reports feeling isolated in his family, he was unable or unwilling to maintain contact with his relatives when he was living rough, and he uses extremely sexually offensive language when he feels threatened. It seems that he has many psychological problems and may have suffered a considerable degree of neglect.

Nat has been under social work supervision for eight months following excessive truancy from school. He moved to another school and did well for three months before truanting again. He lives with his mother and his sister, who is sixteen and unemployed. She has a boyfriend whom Nat describes as violent and a member of a gang. His father left the family home and moved in with a new partner last December while Nat was living on the streets. Both parents are unemployed and in poor health. His mother suffers from depression and sleep disorders. Nat absconded and lived rough for several weeks at the end of last year to escape threats from a gang to which he belonged. He said he had often been forced to commit car thefts. He claims to have witnessed arson and extreme incidents of torture of members of the community. He also claims his cat was killed as a way of pressuring him to comply with the gang's activities. He said he began to use drugs and alcohol as a way to cope with the stress of the events. He absconded after receiving a serious threat to his life because he had a drug debt. He does not recognise that street life holds many dangers but he is afraid to go home where he will be exposed to the dangers of the gang and he wants to be in secure accommodation.

The family members have been reticent about the gang's activities but the police report that their house has often been used by the gang as a base. It is not clear to what extent Nat's relatives are also being intimidated but they are reluctant to recognise the seriousness of Nat's fears.

Stage 2: What Options Are There?

The social worker identified six options:

1. Remaining in the secure unit and developing a safety plan to facilitate an eventual return to the community.
2. Moving to a non-secure residential unit linked to the secure unit.
3. Placement in a foster home.
4. Returning home to mother and sister with the family being offered support and a safety plan being developed.
5. Placement with his brother, Ben, age nineteen; they have been offered support and a safety plan has been developed.
6. Placement with his father and his aunt; they have been offered support and a safety plan has been developed.

Stage 3: What Information Is Needed To Help Make the Choice?

More information is needed about Nat's past and present experiences of family life but his relatives' reluctance to co-operate, possibly through fear of punishment from the gang, makes it very hard to do a thorough assessment.

Stage 4: What Are the Likely/Possible Consequences of Each Option?

For brevity, the options are clustered in three sets, reflecting their similarities. With options (1) and (2), three initial, possible consequences were identified and their subsequent outcomes considered. (i) Nat co-operates with developing a safety plan and gradually moves back to the community. This in turn might be a success or failure. (ii) Nat refuses to co-operate with staff and is eventually moved to another placement where he might or might not settle well. (iii) Nat runs away. He might, then, cope or get into serious trouble.

In option (3) Nat might settle well in a foster placement, or he might abscond, or the placement might break down.

Options (4), (5) and (6), all family placements, were considered together. All held the possibility of Nat and the relevant family members co-operating or not with a safety plan and of that plan's being successful or unsuccessful.

Stage 5: How Probable Is Each Consequence?

Nat's wish to be away from his family and community at present make it likely that he will co-operate best with any option that respects his wishes. He has not tried to abscond from the secure unit, feels safe there, has shown a willingness to trust staff and has been a willing participant in developing his safety plan. His co-operation is vital to the success of any plan. If he absconds and lives rough again, then, on the basis of his past history, he is highly likely to suffer some degree of harm. The residential unit linked to the secure unit offers many of the same advantages but only if he co-operates with the move.

A successful placement in a foster home looks unlikely at present since Nat has many serious problems that he has only just begun to address. He would be very challenging for any carer.

If Nat returns to family his, their current attitude to his problems makes them unlikely to help him effectively in dealing with the threats from the gang and he is, therefore, highly likely to abscond again and face the dangers of living rough.

Stage 6: What Are the Pros and Cons of Each Consequence (i.e. What Is Their Expected Utility)?

A longer stay in a secure unit, although likely to be therapeutically effective, has several negatives. It is very expensive, it restricts Nat's liberty, and the law requires it should be used only if there is no alternative. All the alternatives carry the risk of Nat's absconding except the residential unit. Although this is not secure, it meets many of Nat's requests and would, legally and ethically, be preferable to the secure unit.

Stage 7: The Final Decision

The following decision tree (Figure 7.8) has been fully worked out as an illustration but, in practice, the social worker was able to rule out all the possible family placements at an early stage. It became clear that the risk of absconding was so high and entailed such bleak consequences that, unless the family altered their attitude to Nat's fears, there was little chance of these placements being successful. Equally, the foster placement was ruled out because of how challenging Nat's behaviour was. The decision came down to a choice between the secure unit and the residential unit. They had different pros and cons. The secure unit offered the lowest chance of Nat's absconding but all its consequences had a lower utility value than those of the residential unit not just because of the extra cost but also because it infringed his civil liberties. The final decision was that Nat should be introduced to the residential unit and then be moved there. If he failed to settle and engage with the staff, consideration could be given to his returning to the secure unit.

Case Two

Stage 1: What Decision Is To Be Made?

Chloe, age six, has cerebral palsy and suffers from significant delay in emotional, cognitive, and social attainments although she has previously been assessed as of average intelligence. She has difficulty in walking and uses a wheelchair most of the time. Her personal care skills are limited. She is an only child and lives with her mother, Ms Smith, who is unmarried. Although the cerebral palsy contributes to her developmental delay, professionals have concluded that her mother's level of care is also a significant factor. Education, health and social services have all been offering extensive services for both Chloe and her mother but these are having inadequate effect and it is considered that her mother is

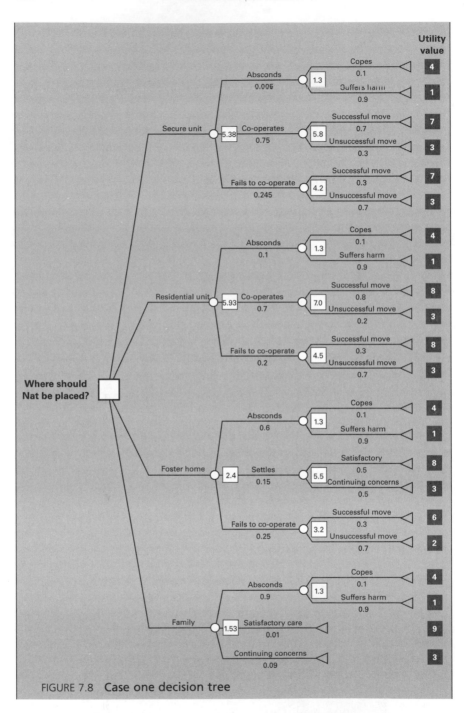

FIGURE 7.8 **Case one decision tree**

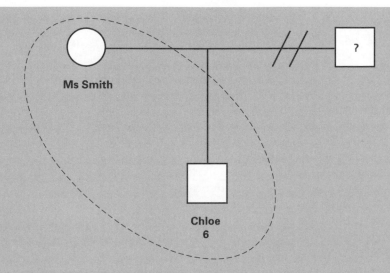

FIGURE 7.9 **Case two family genogram**

sabotaging efforts to help Chloe. The decision is whether to continue with the imperfect package of care or to choose a new strategy in helping Chloe.

This small family unit is socially isolated from relatives. No information is available about Chloe's father. Ms Smith has one sister, with whom she has quarrelled. Ms Smith has diagnosed herself as suffering from depression but receives no treatment for it. She does not work and has few social contacts.

Despite making statements about being devoted to her daughter, she does not seem to spend much time in contact with her. At her request, she has regular respite weekends. Chloe has a care package of forty hours home tuition and Bobath therapy (a treatment programme for cerebral palsy) per week. Ms Smith has repeatedly sabotaged or ended service provision by taking a personal dislike to the staff involved and making formal complaints about them. She is sometimes extremely complimentary about one staff member and very disparaging of another. This appears to be so arbitrary that it is difficult to plan for the family's need consistently. She frequently expresses her belief, in very emotive and extreme terms, that she is being attacked or persecuted by professionals. She does not recognise any failings within herself, which makes it difficult to address her complaints realistically. The social worker, using Kleinian theory, judged that Ms Smith operated continually in a paranoid-schizoid position, splitting her good and bad experiences, including her love for and hostility to her child, and projecting the bad onto professionals. Everybody uses defence mechanisms to some degree but it is the extent to which Ms Smith uses them that is unhealthy (this is a very short précis of the social worker's detailed assessment). Much time and effort has gone into helping Ms Smith but with no noticeable improvement of working relationships. She has refused any therapy directed at herself and her mental health problems.

It is a concern that an unhealthy parent-child relationship is hindering Chloe's development to a significant degree, over and above the difficulties already experienced with her disability. The year before, she had attended a mainstream school part-time but her mother decided this was not meeting her specialist needs. She had asked for Chloe's placement at the specialist Peto Institute but the local authority refused to fund this. She therefore agreed to a care package of home-based Bobath therapy and tutoring. The child seems to have a poor attachment to her mother, who seems to find it hard to tolerate her company. This is affecting Chloe's emotional, social and cognitive development.

Stage 2: What Options Are There?

The social worker has identified six options:

1. Therapy for the mother.
2. Full-time accommodation.
3. No change in current service provision.
4. Regular weekend respite carers coming to the home.
5. Frequent short respite breaks in a residential unit.
6. Regular weekend foster care.

The last three are clustered into one option, at this stage, since they all represent ways of increasing the level of support and are likely to have similar consequences and values. For legal reasons, withdrawal of services is not an option.

Stage 3: What Information Is Needed To Help Make the Choice?

A psychiatric assessment of the mother's mental health is the most important gap in the current assessment but she has refused to allow this.

Stage 4: What Are the Likely/Possible Consequences of Each Option?

For all options, the consequences are clustered into three categories: continuing moderate harm to the child's development, deterioration in the level of care, and improved life chances.

Stage 5: How Probable Is Each Consequence?

The probability of seeing improvement in Chloe's development and life chances seemed very low for every option except full-time accommodation. Past experience of working with Ms Smith made the social worker conclude that any plan that required her active participation was unlikely to be implemented effectively. Even if she agreed to try therapy, she would find it very hard to stay in it. Additional respite might have a short-term benefit but, given her history, no relationship with a substitute carer was likely to last long and so this would not provide Chloe with the consistency she needs. The possibility of matters deteriorating seemed equally as probable as the situation staying much the same.

Stage 6: What Are the Pros and Cons of Each Consequence (i.e. What Is Their Expected Utility)?

The outcome with the highest value would be that Ms Smith responded well to therapy and her relationships with Chloe and the professionals improved with a subsequent improvement in the child's development generally. This would leave Chloe in the birth family with consistent access to the health, education and social services she needs. For the options where she stayed at home, improvement was not given such a high value, because it would be at the cost of continued strained, stressful and time-consuming relationships with the professionals. Improvement in full-time care was also given a lower value since it involved breaking up the birth family. On reflection, the social worker came to the conclusion that there was little difference in value between her two other outcomes, deterioration and continuation of the current level of harm that Chloe was suffering, because, in the long term, the latter would be very damaging to her life chances.

Stage 7: The Final Decision

The social worker's final decision was that only full-time accommodation would substantially improve Chloe's life chances.

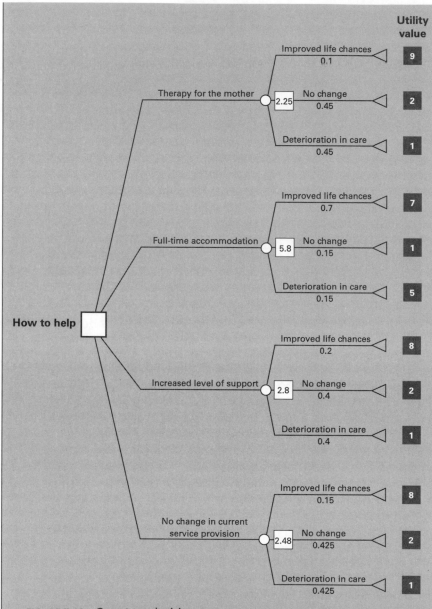

FIGURE 7.10 **Case two decision tree**

However, she thought it unlikely that her mother would agree to a voluntary arrangement, despite her frequent demands that Chloe be taken away from her for short periods. Therefore, plans would need to be made for starting care proceedings.

CONCLUSION

Decision making is both intellectually and emotionally challenging. There is great disparity between the prescriptive methods of decision theorists and the models of decision making developed by those who have studied how people make decisions in real-life situations. Both strands of research have something to offer child protection work.

The descriptive models of decision making highlight the importance of experience in helping professionals make sense of a problem and decide on what to do. This has implications for training and organising work. Students need to be exposed to numerous case examples to build up their intuitive skills in recognising patterns and learning how problems are likely to progress. This could be achieved not only through direct work experience but also by using case vignettes and videos to maximise the range of learning opportunities.

Speed is the greatest strength of intuitive methods in making choices and, in many child protection scenarios, speed is essential. There are, however, other scenarios where speed is less important but optimising the decision is the priority and the cost of making a mistake is high. In these circumstances, decision theory offers a framework to help make the reasoning process explicit and systematic. It offers a way of deciding which course of action is likely to maximise the desirable, and minimise the undesirable, consequences.

The decision framework need not be followed in detail in every situation. Professionals can use it to sketch an overview of the decision they are facing and then concentrate on the problematic elements. It encourages people to make their intuitive reasoning explicit and then think it through more thoroughly. It does not remove subjectivity from the process and two rational people will not necessarily agree on what to do. It does, however, help them to identify where and why they disagree. Its greatest strength perhaps, in these days of public outrage when something goes wrong, is that it enables professionals to provide a clear, defensible account of how they reached a decision.

SUMMARY

- Intuitive decision making relies heavily on experience, pattern recognition and finding a 'good enough' option.
- Decision theory is useful when (i) there is sufficient time, (ii) the cost of error is high, and (iii) the reasoning needs to be open and accountable.
- Decision theory encourages people to think of more options.

- Decision theory encourages people to think beyond the immediate consequence of choosing one option to its possible/probable outcomes.
- Decision theory separates the two values: the probability of an outcome's occurring and its utility value – its desirability or undesirability.
- Decision theory clarifies what needs to be known to make an informed decision.

8

minimising mistakes

The single most important factor in minimising errors is to admit that you may be wrong. At an intellectual level, everyone in child protection knows how fallible knowledge is. With the best intentions and the best training, understanding of what goes on in someone else's mind and ability to see into the future are limited. Emotionally, however, it is a different story. Research has shown time and again how resistant people are to changing their mind. Once they have formed a judgement, they become very attached to it and avoid seeing or accepting any evidence that challenges it (Janis and Mann, 1977; Nisbett and Ross, 1980; Kahneman et al., 1990; Baron, 1994).

This intransigence is reflected in cultural attitudes to mistakes. A change of mind may be mocked as a sign of weakness. 'Good' thinkers are often seen as people who are steadfast and resilient in defending their views when they might, more accurately, be called stubborn and pig-headed. The problem is that people tend to confuse different types of error. Of course, it is a sign of weakness to give up a belief just because of being overwhelmed by someone with a stronger personality. It is a sign of intelligence, though, to revise a judgement when given new information that shows it was misguided. Professional errors are also of two significantly different types. Some are inevitable given the fallibility of the knowledge base. Judgements and decisions can be made only on the knowledge and evidence available at the time. Some mistakes, however, are avoidable: a competent professional should have acted differently. Distinguishing the two types of error is essential for defining 'good practice' in child protection and it is a theme of this chapter.

Much of the research on human reasoning focuses on individuals and tends to lay the blame on them for any biases or inadequacies in their intellectual skills (e.g. Kahneman et al., 1990). Those who have been studying natural decision making dispute this and argue that it underestimates the importance of the context in which the individual is operating. Woods et al. (1993) claim that if we were to study errors by understanding the information available to individuals, the goals being pursued, and their level of experience, we would stop blaming the individual but see how the wider system contributed to the error and how change at these levels would be the most effective strategy for reducing mistakes.

Therefore, in this chapter, I shall look at ways of minimising errors by starting with the wider context before moving on to the individual. At the widest level, society's attitudes to child protection workers set the scene in terms of how much they value them, how well they resource the work, how critical they are of any mistakes, and how realistic they are in what they expect them to be able to achieve. The child protection service and then the particular agency reflect these social attitudes and have a culture that affects how competently professionals can perform their task. This chapter first examines the agency's impact on reasoning, then considers what the individual can do to reduce the chances of making mistakes, and finally looks at the particular effects of making decisions in groups.

THE AGENCY CONTEXT

What can the agency do to foster good reasoning skills in its staff? There are three main sets of factors: having staff with the appropriate knowledge and skills, providing sufficient resources to leave time for critical thinking, and offering skilled supervision.

Knowledge and Skills

An important question is whether the right people have been appointed for the job. Do they have training that is adequate for the tasks facing them? Do they have the right level of experience? Staffing crises in many countries lead employers to lower their standards in making appointments. For example, in Britain ten years ago, it was generally considered that a newly qualified social worker should not be expected to be the lead worker on a case of serious child abuse. Nowadays, the level of staff shortages in many areas is making it impossible to keep to this principle. There is also a growing international mobility of social workers so that many are appointed who have little knowledge of the local legislation and limited understanding of the culture. The appointment of people who lack relevant training or experience may not be a problem as long as employers recognise that they need to provide extra training and good supervision, and do not have unrealistic expectations of what their staff can do.

Resources

Do staff have the resources needed to work to a good level? At the practical level, the quality of the physical environment affects people's ability to function. Noisy, crowded, unheated or badly ventilated offices make it harder for people to concentrate. Adequate administration and computer back-up are also important factors in enabling staff to concentrate on the difficult aspects of their work. In one social work office I visited recently, staff were using the official forms for making plans about individual children in public care. They rarely referred to these plans, however, in their subsequent work with the child. The reason was that they had to be handwritten and then sent to the typing pool and there was a six-month delay in getting them back. The plans were, therefore, not physically available to be consulted.

Wattam and Thorpe (1996) have studied the layout of duty child protection team offices and how it affected the tasks being carried out. They identified a number of factors that hindered or enhanced the workers' performance. There was considerable scope for technological innovations to simplify and streamline the process of responding to a referral, such as easy access to computer records, or simple measures like telephone equipment that has redial facilities and allow 'hands off' conversations. Overcrowded offices and shortage of equipment or support staff hampered the workers' performance, occupying their time with trivial tasks. If practical constraints mean that it takes considerable time to obtain information, practitioners are more likely to feel pressured into making judgements and decisions on the basis of inadequate evidence.

The biggest factors affecting how much time professionals have to deal with a family are size and complexity of caseload. Yet time is essential if people are to reflect, examine their reasoning critically, and obtain the best possible range of information to inform their decisions.

Supervision

The final aspect of the agency's contribution to good reasoning is supervision. It is widely acknowledged that professionals need supervisory help to be objective about their work. In British inquiries after children's deaths, it is again and again stressed that front-line workers tend to get so close to a family that they need assistance in standing back and reviewing their work. Government guidance makes it clear that supervision should be available to front-line workers:

> Supervision should include scrutinising and evaluating the work carried out, assessing the strengths and weaknesses of the practitioner, and providing coaching, development, and pastoral support. Supervisors should be available to practitioners as an important source of advice and expertise. (Department of Health, 1999: 109)

Yet research in Britain has repeatedly found that agencies are economising on the amount of supervision time available. Moreover, there has been a distinct and substantial shift in recent years of the focus of supervision to *management* oversight of the case, ensuring that procedures are being followed correctly (Rushton and Nathan, 1996). This is at the expense of providing emotional support and supervision of the professional task. It is well recognised that child protection work can arouse powerful feelings in staff and affect their rationality (Morrison, 1990). They can over-identify with either the child or the parents; they may become punitive or distant as defence mechanisms against the emotional impact. One inquiry into a child death concluded that supervision is needed to 'help the worker recognise the effects achieved by emotions being beamed out by the family; many emotions and reactions are contagious' (London Borough of Greenwich, 1987). In relation to supervising the professional task, practitioners need assistance not only with ensuring they have the relevant information but also in being critical of their reasoning. Supervisors need to help them distance themselves from their assessments and to review and evaluate the reliability of their information and the soundness of their judgements. A more detailed account of how a supervisor can help minimise errors will be given in the following section on individual reasoning.

An agency's failure to provide a work environment that supports good practice is most dramatically illustrated in staff burnout. In the human services, burnout has been defined in terms of three dimensions: emotional exhaustion, depersonalisation (or cynicism), and reduced personal accomplishment (Maslach et al., 2001).

Exhaustion is the principal and most obvious manifestation. It prompts people to distance themselves emotionally and cognitively from their work, presumably to reduce the feeling of being overloaded. This cynicism can lead to grossly distorted assessments of clients or users (Rumgay and Munro, 2001). Depersonalisation or cynicism is an attempt to put distance between oneself and the service users by actively ignoring the features that make them unique and engaging people; their demands become more manageable when they are seen as impersonal objects of work. A work situation with chronic, overwhelming demands that makes people feel exhausted and cynical is likely to erode workers' sense of effectiveness; at the same time, being exhausted and cynical will make them less effective.

Burnout is a response to the work context and research has found the following factors to be important (Maslach et al., 2001):

- Feeling that there is too much work to do in the time available is consistently related to burnout.
- Experiencing the conflict of having to meet competing demands in the job is stressful.
- Also stressful is 'role ambiguity' – not being given enough information to do the job well.
- A lack of social support contributes to job burnout, especially support from supervisors. People's degree of control over their work is also important. Getting feedback on what has been done, being involved in decision making, and feelings of autonomy are all positive experiences.

- Working intensively with people in either a caregiving or teaching role is emotionally challenging and this feature of child protection work can be expected to contribute to burnout.

A recent study in the USA and the Netherlands of burnout among social service workers, comparing them with other workers, found that levels of cynicism were high in the USA but average in the Netherlands, suggesting there is a cultural component to it (Schaufeli and Enzmann, 1998).

People do not just react to their work setting but also bring their own personality to it. However, research has found that individual characteristics, such as youth and being unmarried, have some significance but are not as important as situational factors in producing burnout. It should therefore be regarded, for the most part, as a social, not an individual, phenomenon.

In terms of encouraging good thinking habits, perhaps the most important factor is the least tangible one of cultural attitude. Are people criticised if they say they have altered their assessment of a family? Is there an underlying assumption that a 'good' worker is superhuman and gets it right first time? Being critical of one's own practice is emotionally hard. If, at the same time, staff feel criticised and looked down on by their seniors, then the temptation is to close one's eyes and be uncritical.

THE INDIVIDUAL

Most research on human reasoning has concentrated on individual thinkers rather than their context. Researchers measure performance against the standards set by formal logic, probability theory, and decision theory and find that people tend to deviate from these models. Instead, they make great use of 'heuristics', shortcuts, approximations or rules of thumb that simplify the reasoning process. These heuristics methods work well enough in daily life but lead to predictable and persistent biases and errors. Some writers present the use of heuristics as a defect, evidence of how far people fall short of an ideal rationality. However, it can be argued that they are highly functional. Human brains have a finite capacity and heuristics, by offering a way of simplifying complex cognitive processes, allows people to perform necessary tasks within the bounds of their ability and in a reasonable time. It would be inefficient to spend a long period of time on every judgement or decision whatever its importance. The time and effort saved compensates for the persistent biases heuristics produces.

However, child protection work is not concerned with trivial matters and so a higher level of accuracy is needed when making judgements and decisions with far-reaching consequences. It is unrealistic to aim at *avoiding* these biases: they seem to be an unavoidable aspect of the way human brains work. Professionals can aim only to *detect* and *minimise* them.

THE RANGE OF EVIDENCE USED

Certain types of information come to mind much more readily than others and so are more 'available' to the professional when reasoning about a family. Consequently, a biased range of evidence is used in making assessments and decisions with a predictable impact on accuracy. The kind of details people think of most easily are

- Vivid, not dull
- Concrete, not abstract
- Emotion laden, not neutral
- Recent, not in the past
- First impressions are an exception and have an enduring impact.

This means that, in assessing a family, workers are likely to give undue weight to information that has been presented to them in a vivid way. The verbal communications from a doctor will stick in the mind more persistently than the dull notes in old records. Details with emotional content – a claim that the child was screaming in fear, for instance – will overshadow a bland report that school attendance has been satisfactory. Indeed, one highly emotive item can dominate discussions. Any particularly horrific or macabre form of abuse will engage people's imagination and attention to the exclusion of the commonplace. In the recent case of a child's death in England, a little girl had been made to sleep in the bath in a black plastic bin liner. This was heavily reported in every newspaper far more than the miserable minutiae of her everyday life. People who are present at a discussion of a family will be able to present their information and their opinions more influentially than those who only make a written or telephoned report.

> At a case conference on a three year old child who had suffered chronic, moderate physical abuse, participants were optimistic that the parents were making good progress. They read a medical report from a paediatrician that said that recent injuries seen on the child could not be non-accidental. The conference notes do not show that any effort was made to discredit this judgement; it seems merely to have been ignored. The conference concluded 'there have been no injuries to cause concern'. (Wandsworth Area Child Protection Committee, 1990)

The bias towards using current information has been found in research on child protection (Social Services Inspectorate, 1993; Farmer and Owen, 1995; Munro, 1999). Professionals tend to get absorbed in present-day issues and fail to stand back and place them in the long-term history of the family. Farmer and Owen's (1995) study of case conferences found that current information gained from police and social work investigations dominated discussion. Little attention was paid to getting a picture of past history from the records. The emphasis was on giving detailed verbal accounts of what had just happened, and what family members had said and how they had reacted to the investigation. Parents' reactions to professionals at this stage were interpreted as representative of the quality of their parenting normally, without any effort to check their past behaviour or consider how the peculiarities of the situation might affect their responses.

The failure to look at history makes it easy to overlook patterns of behaviour yet these are often the most reliable warning that matters are escalating or the situation is deteriorating again.

Stephanie Fox had been taken into public care at a year old after a long series of minor to moderate physical injuries. Her father had had an older child in a previous relationship who had suffered serious physical abuse, with many fractured bones. He had been removed from home briefly, then returned to his parents' care while they attended a residential family centre. Professionals thought they were making good progress and planned to discharge them but the baby then choked to death on his own vomit. The verdict was death by natural causes. A year after Stephanie was removed from home, her father and his new partner agreed to go to another residential family centre where Stephanie was returned to them and, six weeks later, twin girls were born. There was growing optimism among professionals about the parents' improvement as a result of therapy and the family left the centre eight months later. The family continued to be monitored and optimism prevailed. Efforts by nursery staff to raise the level of concern because of the number of bruises seen on Stephanie were unsuccessful. The public inquiry found that a total of forty injuries, bruises and burns, were reported, ten to the twins and thirty to Stephanie; twenty four were bruises to her head. She died of head injuries. Each report of injury had been treated in isolation; the parents' explanations were accepted, and the injury was discounted. Professionals, therefore, failed to see the full picture and the pattern of injury. They also failed to notice the similarity to the history of the eldest child who had been abused and later died of natural causes. (Wandsworth Area Child Protection Committee, 1990)

First impressions are one element of the past that has enduring impact. It is well known that people make swift appraisals of anyone new that they meet (Jones et al., 1968; Dawes, 1988). Those initial impressions influence how any new information about them is interpreted. It has been shown that job interviewers form a judgement about a candidate within the first minute or so and spend the rest of the interview trying to confirm that impression (Sutherland, 1992). Since this initial belief is based on very little evidence, it should be treated as a very tentative hypothesis but research suggests that people have undue confidence in it, paying most attention to evidence that supports it, and ignoring or devaluing details that contradict it.

John and Barbara Aukland had three children under four years of age. John was unemployed and had anxiety problems. The family were known to social services and deemed to be mildly problematic. A new social worker took on the case and his first impression of John had been that he was a pleasant, well meaning, but rather nervous man. His wife, Barbara, created a quite different, adverse, impression. She seemed a poor housewife and mother, apathetic and of low intelligence. When Barbara left the family home, taking one child, a two year old daughter with her, she warned professionals that she was worried about the safety of the other two children. She said that John had been violent to her on several occasions. Social workers dismissed her claims as malicious and persuaded her to return the daughter to John since she herself had no suitable place for the child to live. Within weeks, he had killed that child, and the post mortem found a hundred marks of violence, of varying ages, on her body. The public inquiry into the death decided that professionals' first impressions had had a major influence on the way they interpreted new evidence, being inclined to believe John's testimony and disbelieve Barbara's.

One fact that might have been expected to shake their benign opinion of John was that he had been convicted of the manslaughter of his first born child at the age of nine weeks. He had served a prison sentence for this. John told social workers the death was an accident and hinted that Barbara was implicated. They believed him without checking the police or social service records which would have painted a quite different picture. John also had a record of violence to his wife, his parents, and his sister. Again, social workers believed his denials, rejecting the wife's evidence, and failing to check with the probation service who could have provided clear details. (DHSS, 1975)

In attempts to counteract this bias in the range of information used, frameworks for assessment and checklists are crucial in reminding practitioners of the full variety of sources of evidence they should be considering. However, knowledge of the patterns of human bias helps draw attention to the types of data likely to be overlooked intuitively. It is a reminder to be particularly thorough and systematic in checking these less memorable points.

Records have a crucial part to play. Practitioners need to make a clear, detailed record of events so that past history is available to be scrutinised. Patterns can be detected only if practitioners have written down a precise account of what has happened. Certain ways of recording information make it easier to get an overview of a family. The Bridge Child Care Consultancy, who have done a number of inquiries into child deaths, compile a case history chart from the case records to make the following information more accessible for analysis:

- Date
- Time
- Separation/move/change
- Other significant events
- Child's development, including illness/injuries
- What the child says and the impact of this
- Whether any inquiries have been made about the child's risk status
- The source of the information.

This allows the reader to see correlations between events, the level of professional involvement, and the number and type of concerns. (See, for example, BCCCS, 1995.)

If there is concern about physical abuse because of a number of possible minor injuries, an injuries chart makes it very easy to get a full picture of the extent of abuse. In the case of Stephanie Fox, mentioned above, a new social worker took on the case shortly before Stephanie died and began such a chart. If it had been filled in for the whole period she was at home, showing all forty injuries and their alleged causes, the sheer number and repetitiveness of them might have led people at the case conferences to question their optimism about the parents and their willingness to accept the parents' explanations of each injury.

CLINGING TO BELIEFS

The single most pervasive bias in human reasoning is that people like to hold onto their beliefs. It has been commented upon throughout history and is amply demonstrated in psychological research (Bacon, 1620; Janis and Mann, 1977; Nisbett and Ross, 1980). It has a devastating impact in child protection work in that professionals hold onto their beliefs about a family despite new evidence that challenges them. It can be equally harmful whether they are over- or underestimating the degree of risk to the child. They may continue to believe parents are doing well even though there are successive reports of the child's being distressed or injured. Innocent parents wrongly judged abusive can face the frustrating and frightening experience of being unable to shake the professionals' conviction however much counter-evidence they produce.

People employ a number of ways of not recognising evidence that challenges their beliefs:

- Avoidance
- Forgetting
- Rejecting
- Reinterpreting.

Avoidance is most apparent in what evidence is collected or noticed when checking assessments or monitoring progress.

> Leanne White's neighbours made an allegation that she was being abused. A duty social worker followed up the referral, making some checks with other professionals and a home visit. She concluded the allegation was unsubstantiated. When two further sets of neighbours made independent allegations, she did not follow them up because she assumed they were also unsubstantiated. (Nottinghamshire Area Child Protection Committee, 1994)

Jasmine Beckford was rehabilitated with her mother and stepfather after having been physically abused. When her social worker judged that all was going well and the risk to Jasmine was dropping, she reduced the frequency of home visits and failed to collect information from others, such as the school, who were in contact with the family and could have presented data at odds with this optimistic assessment. (London Borough of Brent, 1985)

If the parents are thought to be co-operating well and they tell professionals the child is attending school regularly, there may seem to be no need to ask the school about her attendance. But, by assuming the parents are truthful and, therefore, not checking their word, professionals fail to get evidence that shows they are lying.

Forgetting as a way of overlooking counter-evidence is more likely to happen the more memories, rather than written records, are relied on to check beliefs. If parents are thought to be neglectful, the memory will easily and spontaneously throw up details and images of the behaviour that led to this conclusion. Pictures of the children looking grubby, cold or sad will leap to mind, but memories of home visits when the children looked clean and warm, or the house was in good order, will not be so readily thought of. The word 'neglect' does not trigger a search through the memory banks for 'non-neglect' evidence, but only for corroborative data. In the case of Stephanie Fox that I mentioned earlier, the paediatrician's written report that was read at the beginning of the conference was not discounted in any way. It seems just to have been forgotten by the time it came to an optimistic conclusion.

There are often plausible grounds for *rejecting* counter-evidence in child protection work. There are many reasons why parents accused of being abusive might lie to professionals. Neighbours and relatives, too, can be dishonest, acting out of malice and spite.

It is a standard element of good practice (at least in theory) to interview the children in a case, although their testimony can be unreliable. Their youth may mean that they do not fully understand what is being discussed. They may be scared of the reaction if they tell the truth and say their parents are abusive. Sadly, in my study of inquiry reports (Munro, 1999), I found that children were rarely interviewed and, when they were, their evidence was rejected if it conflicted with the interviewer's point of view. In the ten reports where interviews with children are analysed, seven cases involved children who corroborated their parents' account of their injuries as accidental and said that they were not being abused. In all cases, their statements reinforced the professional's belief about the family and they were believed. In one report, it was unclear what the truth was. In the other six, the inquiries concluded that the children had been lying and had, indeed, been abused. In three cases, the children claimed that they were being abused, evidence that challenged the current, benign assessment of the parents. In all three cases, they were not believed. The inquiries decided, with hindsight, that they had all been telling the truth.

The awkward testimony of other professionals can also be discounted on the grounds that they are inexperienced or not trained as well or as highly as one's own profession in this particular issue. Professionals of low status are particularly vulnerable to not being taken seriously. Inquiries into child protection cases have repeatedly found that evidence from junior staff – helpers in a day nursery or junior-grade nurses, for example – is readily dismissed when it conflicts with the dominant view.

The strategy of rejecting conflicting evidence is apparent in people's approach to evidence-based practice. There tends to be a differential attitude to research evidence. Studies that support our beliefs are accepted without much scrutiny. Findings that conflict, however, tend to be subject to close analysis and criticism so that results can be dismissed as unreliable and so be ignored (Nisbett and Ross, 1980).

The final strategy for ignoring counter-evidence is *reinterpreting* it to become benign. So much evidence in child protection work involves interpreting behaviour that this strategy can be used extensively. It may be clear that someone has performed a specific behaviour but its meaning can be questioned and reconstrued. Is a mother failing to visit her child in hospital because she lacks appropriate love, or is she put off by the hostile, judgemental attitudes of the nursing staff? Actions are judged against the standards of normality and, again, there is considerable scope for reclassifying something as in line with, or against, the norm. There is, for instance, no precise cut-off point between 'normal' physical chastisement and excessive beating.

BEING MORE CRITICAL

It is easy to identify the ways in which reasoning is faulty. It is not so easy to provide an answer. All of the above strategies are reasonable at times. 'Avoidance' is a negative term but, for practical reasons of time and resources, some limits must be put on what evidence is collected in investigations and assessments. Forgetting irrelevant information is essential to keep thinking clear; the problem is in deciding what is, or is not, relevant. It is irrational to believe everything one is told, so, sometimes, counterevidence is quite rightly rejected as false. Reinterpretation, as well, can be a rational response to new information as well as a means of protecting current beliefs. The trouble is there is no algorithm, no precise set of rules, for weighing up evidence that will always specify one 'right' answer that any rational person must agree to. This is not a problem that is peculiar to child protection or to the study of human behaviour. It applies just as much to appraising theories in the natural as in the social sciences (Munro, 1998).

However, there are better and worse ways of evaluating beliefs. A generalisation based on studying 2000 children is more likely to be reliable than one based on looking at one child only. An assessment of risk derived from a social worker's intuitive impression in one interview is less well founded than an assessment drawing on a large range of evidence. Not only is the range of evidence important but also people's attitudes to it. A critical, open-minded approach is more likely to enable professionals to spot errors and revise their beliefs. It leads people to recognise that they might be mistaken and to look for evidence that might falsify their ideas. It enables them to think of other ways of interpreting the information they have, and to treat rival explanations as worthy of rational consideration.

It is also possible to develop more systematic and rigorous ways of testing intuitions. When speed is a major factor in reasoning, intuitive methods are likely to dominate, but they are not used unquestioningly. People do have ways of checking intuitive thinking and these can be made more stringent. They evaluate an explanation of behaviour by asking if it is 'plausible', whether or not this account rings true as a coherent story of how someone might behave. 'Folk psychology' is extensive and provides a wealth of background knowledge of how people tend to behave in different circumstances and this can be used as a check on explanations. If a mother is considered to be very loving and caring towards her son, does this fit with the observed behaviour? If, for instance, the boy has been injured, allegedly accidentally, and is in hospital, is the mother behaving as would be expected? It cannot be specified in advance exactly how she might be expected to behave because there are several ways that parents cope with this kind of event. But if, for instance, the nurses reported that although she sat by the child's bed she avoided physical contact, this might be puzzling and difficult to reconcile with the image of a caring mother. On investigation, there might be a reasonable explanation that dispelled the uncertainty, such as learning that the child had a skin condition that made contact painful. If no such explanation could be found, this detail of her behaviour would sound an alarm and prompt further questioning of the assumption that she was a caring mother.

Child protection workers can be more systematic in the way they test their ideas. Cannon-Bowers and Salas (2000) use the concept of 'stories' in describing how people reason intuitively about human behaviour, they and argue that people can become more critical by trying to expand the story that surrounds an explanation. Their work aimed at improving critical thinking in naval emergencies, a context that has many similarities to child protection in that it requires officers to make swift estimates of what their opponents are thinking, and to weigh up whether unknown craft are friendly or hostile, and how to respond to them. The training developed by Cannon-Bowers and Salas focuses on making the intuitive assessment more detailed and then systematically testing its adequacy.

When an assessment of an allegation has been made, the professional's understanding can be enhanced by constructing a story around it to flesh out the assessment of the human motivation, speculating about what must have gone before to lead to the person's having this motivation in these circumstances, and about what might happen in the future if this understanding is correct. The story can be tested by comparing what is expected, if it is correct, with what is observed. This is similar to the scientific method of testing a theory by deducing observation statements from it and then seeing if they are correct. However, explanations of human behaviour generally involve probabilities, not certainties. It cannot be specified in advance exactly how people are expected to behave in a specific setting because there are several possibilities, any of which might seem plausible. Some ways of behaving, however, do seem unlikely and so appear to conflict. Behaviour that challenges the story can be dealt with by amending the story to account for this new evidence. If, however, the story keeps needing to be patched up, it starts to look dubious and other explanations must be sought. Professionals need to remain aware that they are working with an unproven assessment and have contingency plans if it turns out they are wrong.

Consider the case of a three-year-old girl admitted to hospital with a fractured arm. The parents, who both accompanied her to casualty, describe how it happened and their account seems vivid and realistic. They seem appropriately distressed and they have acted responsibly in immediately bringing the girl to hospital. After four hours on the ward, nursing staff report that the parents show love and concern and the child seems to find their presence comforting. The doctors confirm that the injury is compatible with the explanation and, moreover, it is a common injury for this age group. By development of the story from the present incident to cover the past (the account of the injury), and the future (their behaviour on the ward), the plausibility of the hypothesis that the parents are telling the truth is increased.

This hypothesis would be questioned, though, if the doctors said that the injury was, in fact, two days old, not new, as the parents claimed. The parents could be asked to account for the delay in seeking help. Maybe they claim that she had a similar fall two days ago and the injury must have happened then. Caring parents would be expected to have noticed and responded to the fact that she was in pain. The parents say she did not show distress until that day and they responded immediately. The plausibility of this can be tested by asking a doctor if it is likely. If the medical opinion is that the injury would have caused immediate distress, it becomes difficult to reconcile this with the belief that the parents have been telling the truth. If they are now confronted with the medical opinion and they persist with their account, it has to be decided whether to investigate further. If they are benign parents, as has been assumed, checks with other professionals should reveal no concerns about their parenting. In this particular case, further investigation revealed that there had been a delay in the parents responding to two other injuries to children in this family and, on each occasion, they had visited a different hospital (at some inconvenience to themselves) so that the frequency of injuries was hidden. By this stage, professionals were seriously questioning the parents' claim that the injuries were all accidental. The difficulty, in practice, is to decide how long to go on checking and when to accept what seems, on the surface, a plausible account.

The use of background knowledge to develop stories about families contributes to the difficulties in working with ethnic diversity. With a culture very unlike their own, people may, quite rightly, lack confidence in weaving a tale around the observed behaviour. One way to cope with this is to accept the parents' account completely and uncritically because of being unsure of what is usual or unusual, or of how behaviours fit together. If hindsight shows this trust in the parents was misplaced, professionals can look very naïve for seeming to have swallowed a strange story.

For example, Mr Jones claimed that he had beaten his sixteen-year-old son severely because he had confessed to homosexual feelings. These were totally unacceptable in their religious culture and the standard way of responding was to beat it out of the boy. The social workers accepted this. Later another member of the father's congregation contacted them and angrily said that, although homosexuality was disapproved of, there was nothing in their religion that endorsed the use of severe physical punishment. He felt insulted that social workers were so ready to accept that his sect had such barbaric practices and pointed out how it conflicted with the rest of their beliefs on how to treat children.

The difficulty of deciding how long to go on being sceptical of a story highlights the importance of being able to discuss it with someone else. It is much easier to take an objective look at one's thinking if it can be shared. Sometimes this will be with a colleague in the office but, for most agencies, the standard practice is to offer supervision. The role of a supervisor is crucial. Not only does it provide the intellectual challenges to help practitioners stand back and be critical of their work but also it provides the secure setting in which they can face this emotionally challenging task.

Strategies encouraging a critical approach all involve some way of making people consider that their current view may be wrong. One way is to assume that the opposite belief is true and then to look for evidence to support it. This makes people consider why their current view might be wrong. Koriat et al. (1980) undertook a psychological study aimed at helping people reduce their overconfidence in their first judgements and found this was the most effective strategy. They suggest it may be successful because it makes people address their memory in a different way than just asking them to examine the strength of the case for their belief. It entails looking for information to support the opposing view rather than simply to challenge the existing view, harnessing the general tendency to find it easier to think of information that supports a belief than of facts that conflict with it. The worker who believes a child is lying could try to make a case for claiming she is truthful, and vice versa.

This strategy can be even more powerful when it is done with the help of someone else who adopts the role of devil's advocate. The devil's advocate works from the premise that the assessment is wrong and, like a barrister in a court of law, tries to find weaknesses in the case and produce rival pictures of what might have happened. This technique helps to uncover hidden assumptions in a story and to open people's eyes to alternative interpretations of the evidence. It also helps to identify ways that judgements can be tested further.

GROUP REASONING

Many important judgements and decisions in child protection work are made in a group context. Groups have clear strengths in providing a range of information and of professional expertise. Each of the various professionals who know a family – doctors, nurses, social workers, teachers and police officers – has a partial picture of particular family members in particular contexts. By pooling their resources, they can construct a more detailed and reliable assessment of what is going on. However, groups are vulnerable to their own biases that lead to distorted reasoning. Their biggest failing is a desire to avoid conflict. Janis (1982) describes this bias as 'groupthink':

> A mode of thinking that people engage in when they are deeply involved in a cohesive in-group, when members' striving for unanimity overrides their motivation to realistically appraise alternative courses of action (groups tend to make consensus decisions – there's a lot of pressure to conform).

The intensity of people's reluctance to challenge the group consensus has been shown in psychology research. Experiments have been run where a volunteer has gone into a room with eight other supposed volunteers. The experimenter has asked them all to look at two cards: one shows one line, and the other has three lines. He asks them to say which one is the same length as the single line on the other card. Little does the volunteer know that all the others are stooges and deliberately choose the wrong line. Does the volunteer disagree? Only a quarter have the courage to trust their senses and disagree, and they get very nervous and hesitant as they do so. The rest go along with the consensus view. Some decide there must be something wrong with their eyesight to explain the discrepancy but most just think the majority must be right and convince themselves it is the right answer. It does not take much support to give people the confidence to differ. If just one of the stooges gives the correct answer, most of the volunteers will agree with that person. This may be because they then see that they will not be rejected or ridiculed if they disagree with the others.

There is considerable evidence of the low level of disagreements at group discussions of child protection cases (Farmer and Owen, 1995; Birchall and Hallett, 1995; Bell, 1999). Corby studied 25 cases of child abuse and attended their case conferences. He concluded that:

> The overall picture is one of underlying confusion and disagreement which rarely evidenced itself in open conflict. (1987: 68)

Oddly, the tendency of groups to reach consensus does not lead to middle-of-the-road decisions but to 'extreme' ones; that is, the group will shift to one extreme or the other of being very cautious or being very risky (Moscovici and Zavalloni, 1969). Thus, a group assessing the level of risk a child is at will be more likely to reach agreement around a high-or low-risk assessment than a moderate one.

Janis (1982) identified three major causes of groupthink with respective sub-divisions:

Type I. Overestimation of the Group

1. *An illusion of invulnerability, shared by most or all group members, that leads to overoptimism and excessive risk taking.* This is often fostered by past successes so the more established a group, the more it is vulnerable to this belief.

2. *An unquestioned belief in the group's inherent morality.* This can lead the group to think that any means are justified if they lead to the morally desired conclusion. In a case of alleged organised sexual abuse in Scotland, professionals, particularly the police, were very keen to secure the conviction of the perpetrators and, for the sake of getting uncontaminated forensic evidence, this strongly influenced their plans on how to treat the children. As a result, they do not seem to have addressed the question of whether this treatment was morally acceptable (Scottish Office, 1992).

Type II. Closed-Mindedness

3. *Collective efforts to rationalise or discount warnings.* If the warnings come from people who are not present, the group is particularly likely to find a way of discounting them.

4. *Stereotyped views of adversaries as too evil to make negotiating worthwhile, or too weak and stupid to pose a serious threat.* Professional groups involved in child protection work often develop negative stereotypes of each other (Birchall and Hallett, 1995), facilitating this strategy for avoiding counter-evidence. In Cleveland, when a large number of children were being diagnosed as sexually abused by paediatricians relying on a controversial 'anal dilatation test', the police officers and a police surgeon became concerned that too much confidence was being placed in the accuracy of this test. Rather than have a rational, professional debate, the difference of opinion led to a breakdown in the relationship between the police and the social services. The director of social services wrote a memo to all staff saying that children were no longer to have second medical examinations performed by the (sceptical) police surgeon (Department of Health, 1988).

Type III. Pressures Towards Conformity

5. *Pressure directed at any group member who dissents from the majority view.* Sometimes, dissent does surface and is then directly silenced.

Farmer and Owen (1995) give a striking example of a police officer at a conference they were observing. A two-month-old boy was taken to hospital by his parents with a bruised and bleeding nose. They said he had fallen out of a chair. Doctors said this explanation was consistent with the injuries. But hospital records showed that the baby's two-year-old sister had, in the past eighteen months, been treated twice, once for a fractured skull and once for a dislocated elbow. Nursery staff had also seen bruising on her in this period. The police inspector thought this history of injuries looked more than accidental. He was firmly stopped by the chair, who said that the parents had given satisfactory explanations every time. Later in the conference, the police officer complained that the police had not been informed at the time of the injury. He was told by the doctor that the injury was not serious enough to justify this. His last effort to raise the level of concern was to ask that the police be informed quickly if there were any more accidents in this family. The chair told him they would only be told if it was serious. He stayed quiet after that.

6. *Self-censorship of deviations from the apparent group consensus.* Members may avoid expressing any counter-opinion or criticism for fear of looking a weak or bad team member. If the group's decision has a tragic outcome, they may feel severe guilt and regret for not having spoken up and voicing their doubts.

7. *A shared illusion of unanimity.* Since dissenters are discouraged from expressing their opinion, others may not be aware there is any disagreement. If counter-opinions are expressed, the group may move quickly onto to other issues so that their full import is not appreciated.

8. *Self-appointed 'mindguards' who protect the group from information that might challenge the group's complacency.* Some members of the group may take it upon themselves to keep others in line with the apparent consensus.

The danger that group judgement and decision making will be vulnerable to the two biases of avoiding conflicting views and tending towards a consensus around an extreme position does not negate the value of groups. Their obvious strength lies in the range of knowledge and expertise they contain. It is possible for them to be run in ways that promote good thinking, characterised by a tolerance of opposing views and a willingness to examine the pros and cons of alternatives, not simply defending one course of action. Janis, from his research, also proposed some measures to protect against groupthink:

1. Group leaders should explicitly encourage dissent and criticism – including criticism of their own position.
2. Group leaders should refrain from stating any personal preferences at the outset – they could let the lowest ranking speak first.

3.   Groups should set up other groups with other leaders to consider the same question (thereby allowing for a comparison of different answers).
4.   Group members should periodically discuss the group's deliberations with trusted associates, and should report these discussions to the group.
5.   Groups should invite outside experts or qualified colleagues to attend the group meetings and should encourage them to challenge the group consensus.
6.   Group should appoint someone in the group to be the official devil's advocate to dissent from the consensus.

One student of mine found the last strategy of appointing an official devil's advocate particularly useful. When she first told her team of the idea, they were very sceptical and reluctant. She persevered and appointed a devil's advocate on a weekly rotation. After a couple of weeks, the group realised the fun of being sanctioned to disagree and started to compete for the role. They also found it led to a more critical and thorough appraisal of their reasoning without threatening the group's cohesion.

The pressure to conform in a group may be particularly strong in child protection work because it leads to a shared responsibility for the decisions made; all present agreed this was the right thing to do. In the event of a tragic outcome, all can feel they have the support of the others and cannot be singled out for blame. However, in a good decision-making context, it should always be possible for people to raise questions and offer alternative ideas.

CONCLUSION

The agency has a fundamental responsibility for providing the work environment that enhances good, critical reasoning. This entails both creating a culture that encourages spending time and effort on thinking and providing the resources to support it. Ensuring that staff have the appropriate level of experience and training is a first step but the agency also needs to provide adequate support, in terms of both technological equipment and administrative back-up so that the front-line workers have the time to do as thorough an investigation as they think is needed and then the time to receive good supervision and critically review what they have been doing.

Groups have particular strengths and weaknesses as decision makers. Sharing the responsibility for important but difficult decisions reduces the pressure on individuals. The wealth of information between them gives a better foundation for any judgement or decision. But this assumes that the full range of information is used. The strong tendency for groups to avoid conflict acts against critical thinking. This has to be guarded against by deliberate efforts on the part of members to develop a critical culture in which people feel they can raise awkward questions without others responding as if they had been personally attacked.

For the individual, the overwhelming problem with human reasoning is that people do not like changing their beliefs. They go to great lengths to avoid the discomfort of having to revise their judgements. There is no simple antidote to this weakness. Child protection workers can be aware only of how they are likely to err and consciously try to counteract it. They are liable to focus on a restricted range of evidence and use one of several techniques for discounting evidence that challenges their ideas. The individual can be more critical by thinking of the intuitive explanation as a kind of story and testing it by thinking it through more thoroughly. What must have happened in the past and what might happen in the future if this account of the behaviour is true? Supervision, though, is essential if professionals are really going to be helped to be more critical, in terms of providing both the intellectual challenge and the emotional encouragement.

A shift to a more critical approach is equivalent to changing from being a barrister to being a detective. A barrister defends one point of view, offering only information that supports it and trying to deny or discredit any challenges thrown at it by the opposing side. A detective is trying to establish the truth and looks diligently for evidence for and against a point of view. There is an openness to new evidence and to rival views and different explanations. The barrister is firmly on one side only. The detective is in the more uncomfortable position of being undecided and looking for the strengths on both sides of an argument. This discomfort, unfortunately, seems to be an unavoidable element of critical practice. Child protection work is intellectually and emotionally challenging.

SUMMARY

- People cannot avoid the biases of human reasoning; they can only hope to detect and minimise them.
- The agency has to ensure that professionals have the right knowledge and skills for the job they are expected to do, the resources and the time to do the job to a good standard, and the supervision to help them be more objective about their reasoning.
- The individual can be more critical of intuitive explanations by trying to develop them into a fuller story and then checking whether past and future events are compatible with it.

- The supervisor can help by taking a devil's advocate position or by asking the practitioner to think of evidence why the opposing point of view might be correct.
- Groups need to beware of 'groupthink' and take steps to encourage critical thinking so that the wealth of information available to them is used.
- Good critical thinking needs to be supported by the work environment. The culture has to welcome and encourage time spent on thinking and allow for this.

9

conclusion

Child protection work makes heavy demands on reasoning skills. With an issue as important as children's welfare, it is vital to have the best standard of thinking that is humanly possible. Mistakes are costly to the child and the family. Overestimating the danger is as harmful as under-estimating it. But there are several features of child abuse that make it difficult to achieve a high level of accuracy in identifying or predicting abuse. There are problems both in developing a reliable body of knowledge and in determining how to use the knowledge and skills that already exist.

Most efforts to improve practice, at present, involve trying to make it more formal and analytic. Empirical research is being funded to increase our understanding and to evaluate practice. Work is increasingly shaped by procedures and guidelines. Assessments are based on frameworks of varying degrees of precision. The underlying assumption is that the more the intuitive skills of the individual can be eliminated from the process, the better the practice.

The case for developing the formal knowledge base of practice and formal aids to reasoning seems indisputable. History provides over-whelming evidence of how persistently misguided people can be. Medicine's past is littered with false beliefs that, at the time, seemed solidly confirmed by clinical experience:

> Historians of medicine inform us that before around 1890 almost everything that physicians did in treatment was either useless or actively harmful. For example, standard procedures included bleeding, purging, and blistering, the first two being harmful, the third irksome, and all useless. (Meehl, 1997: 92)

The development of scientific reasoning has led to a transformation of people's understanding of the world and their ability to manipulate it. It should not, however, be seen as a completely new way of thinking. People do, intuitively, formulate hypotheses and test them, to some extent, against their experience as they build up folk psychology and other beliefs. Science differs in terms of degree, not kind. Its theories are more explicitly formulated; its causal theories are deeper; and scientists have a greater commitment to rigorous testing and looking for evidence to disprove their beliefs. The net effect of these changes of degree has been impressive. Adopting them in efforts to protect children from abuse, therefore, seems highly sensible.

In this book, I have discussed a number of pros and cons in relation to developing formal knowledge. One obstacle is that the core concept of child abuse is socially constructed and evolving. Whether the impact of globalisation will be that societies move towards a greater consensus on human rights and beliefs about child rearing is unknown. Certainly, at present, there is a considerable range of beliefs about what constitutes unacceptable or dangerous parenting. The concept of abuse is also so wide ranging that it is unlikely that any one theory of causation will be adequate. However, although it cannot be hoped to develop any knowledge as universal and reliable as, say, the understanding of measles, this is far from claiming that no progress can be made; it is likely to be made in relation to specific forms of abuse in specific contexts.

Another obstacle to developing a more formal knowledge base is that human behaviour seems to have such a complex causation. This makes it hard to develop precise predictions about how any one person will react in a given context. Child abuse is, fortunately, relatively rare statistically and this creates serious problems in developing accurate diagnostic or predictive tools. They tend to produce very high rates of false positives and false negatives. It is less of a problem if dealing with populations with a high base rate of abuse. There is more likely to be success in developing actuarial tools to use on families already known to cause concern, rather than on trying to screen the whole population for their abuse potential.

However, it is the complexity of human behaviour that merits a more formal approach in assessments and reviews. Intuitively, people are likely to concentrate on some areas and forget others. They are particularly vulnerable to focusing on information that is vivid, concrete, emotion laden, recent, or the first impression. There are obvious merits to a checklist that ensures a wider range of evidence is used in making and reviewing assessments.

The difficulty of creating formal instruments that can accurately predict who will be abusive is not a reason for preferring intuitive risk assessments. Clinical judgement is no better, and there are several reasons for expecting it to be worse, than an actuarial tool. People have very poor skills in dealing with probabilities intuitively and so their predictions are likely to be based on very crude and inaccurate computations of the evidence. Formal tools use statistical formulae to handle the calculations and so, given the same set of information, are going to produce more accurate results than intuition.

The formal analysis of the statistics of making predictions draws attention to the limits of professionals' ability to foretell the future and accurately identify which parents will, or will not, abuse their children. This means that they should treat their practice judgements with caution, knowing how fallible they are. In subsequent work with a family they need to stay aware that they may be wrong. Here, the scientific emphasis on looking for evidence to challenge one's beliefs comes to the fore. Intuitively, people tend to see what confirms their beliefs and ignore or reject conflicting evidence. To counter this, professionals need to make conscious and systematic efforts to check their judgements about a family.

Despite its limitations, a more analytic approach to practice would seem to have much to offer. Yet it still has many opponents. Since many of these are in front-line work, it needs to gain their support to have a significant influence on the quality of practice. Politicians and managers can impose systems and procedures on practitioners but, unless the practitioners use them properly, this will be with only fragmented and limited effect. There is evidence that many front-line workers are resistant to moving away from their customary intuitive approach. They obey orders and complete the prescribed risk assessment frameworks and decision-making aids but retain confidence in their own intuitive reasoning. The introduction of formal aids then becomes an extra burden, not a support.

Why are people so hard to convert to the advantages of analytic thinking? This has long perplexed its advocates. One possibility is that people who prefer intuition are stupid. This explanation is often hinted at, at least in the more tetchy discussions. It seems unlikely, however, given the scale of resistance among front-line workers. It is not just social workers but psychologists, nurses, and teachers who think their intuitive skills are valuable. Resistance is not even just found among the helping professions. The US military spent millions of dollars in the 1970s and '80s developing expensive decision aids for battlefield commanders. Unfortunately, no one would use them, preferring to stick to their intuitive wisdom (Klein, 2000: 7).

A few defend their preference for intuitive thinking by claiming that it is as reliable as science. For most of the twentieth century, science was seen as providing certainty. People had immense confidence in its ability to discover truths about the world. While few philosophers would ever have defended this view, it was widely accepted among the general public. The philosophical arguments against the positivist view of science have now gained widespread currency and people's confidence in science is lessening. Some react by concluding that if science does not offer certainty, it offers nothing, and is no better than any other way of making sense of the world. Therefore, there is no good reason to abandon their preferred methods of empathy and intuition. This is to overstate the implications of abandoning positivism. Empiricism would not claim to achieve certainty but would claim that scientific methods are better at testing and discarding hypotheses than intuitive skills. The history of science and technological advance provides evidence to support this claim. This defence of intuition by rejecting science is not widely accepted nor does it stand up well to critical scrutiny (Munro, 1998).

A more convincing reason for people's resistance is that the formal approach undervalues intuitive skills and, on its own, is not workable.

Some of the advocates of analytic knowledge are extremely critical of intuition. William Grove and Paul Meehl, in criticising clinical psychologists for not using research results, scathingly define clinical experience as 'a prestigious synonym for *anecdotal evidence* when the anecdotes are told by somebody with a professional degree and a license to practice a healing art' (Grove and Meehl, 1996: 302). This seems harsh and grossly overestimates the area of practice for which scientific methods can provide reliable guidance. I have argued in this book that intuitive and analytic skills are needed at different points in practice. The great strengths of intuition are speed and the range of background wisdom it draws on. Formal methods cannot replace intuitive skills in forming relationships with families. Yet the quality of these relationships will have an impact on every subsequent stage in practice: the family's willingness to provide accurate information, to co-operate with professionals, and to be motivated to change. 'Folk psychology' is a somewhat derogatory term for a wealth of background knowledge that enables people to communicate effectively with each other. Formal decision theory, too, has limited practical application. The process of working with a family involves numerous microdecisions that are best dealt with intuitively.

Many of those who want professionals to adopt formal assessment frameworks and decision aids would say that they realise relationship skills are needed to *use* their forms and collect the necessary information from people. However, this is only a lukewarm acceptance. The trouble is that the debate between analytic and intuitive thinking has been polarised for so long that it has been presented as an issue of deciding which is better in some absolute sense. Therefore, people on one side are reluctant to see any good in their opponents' view. The idea of a continuum changes this issue to one of deciding which is better, to what degree, in what context.

A formal assessment framework administered in a coldly bureaucratic way with no interviewing skills should be criticised. It is wrong not just on the technical grounds that it is unlikely to engage the family's co-operation, and so the evidence gathered is likely to be inaccurate and incomplete, but also on the moral grounds that this is not the way to treat fellow human beings. They are not objects but subjects. At the other extreme, if an agency has developed an actuarial tool that has been shown to have a higher accuracy rate than experienced professionals, then, unless professionals can produce some very specific evidence, it is irrational to claim that, despite the evidence, their professional expertise is superior.

This debate about the value of intuition is important. If the strengths of analytic thinking are presented as absolutely superior to practice wisdom and intuition, it is overstating its case and *practitioners know it*. They are aware of the skills needed in calming a terrified child so that she can be asked what has been happening to her. They also know that these are not small background skills behind the serious business of conducting an investigation. They are central to being in a helping profession and relating to people, not machines. In many respects, they are the most challenging and difficult aspects of practice, especially to a novice. The individual's sense of professional development rests to a significant extent on improving intuitive skills, not just on learning law, procedures, and formal theories.

If analytic and intuitive skills are seen as on a continuum, the question becomes one of what relative contribution should each make in the whole child protection process? I want to consider this question in relation to three issues: how empirical research findings are to be integrated into practice, what type of training is needed, and what type of work environment will support good thinking.

DESIGNING AIDS TO PRACTICE

Many of the frameworks and decision aids available at present are only half-heartedly used, if at all, by practitioners, who complain that they conflict with their current ways of working. Some of the complaints depend on what advice is given on using the aids. Guidelines, for example, can be treated as absolute rules that must be obeyed whatever the circumstances. If so, there will be occasions when practitioners can quite rightly point to their ineptness. Guidance on how quickly an initial investigation should be completed, for instance, can be inoperable if a parent is away for a few days or if it is the Christmas period and many of the relevant people are unobtainable.

Assessment frameworks, too, can be presented as guides to what should be covered or as forms that need to be filled in, starting at Page One and going through each question in turn. The latter option gives no consideration to issues about engaging the family's co-operation or being sensitive to their particular needs. In one case, the professional, using a standard format, began the interview with a question about the number of children in the family. Since, as the professional knew, the current crisis had been triggered by the death of one son in a road accident, this question was extremely distressing to the parents, immediately pushing them into talking about this trauma.

Researchers might well say that they never intended their material to be used in such a mechanical fashion and they expect professionals to use their expertise as well as the formal guidance. However, they do not control the work environment and the front-line workers are most influenced by the messages they get from their managers. For many, this message is to follow guidance as if it were a rule. As Stevenson (1999: 94) comments on the scene in the UK:

The problem is that 'a guide', if it is to be followed, needs a climate of professional support which has been shown to be lacking in Social Services

Departments. Rules are therefore perceived to be necessary and the application of bureaucratic modes of enforcement follows.

The problem in the UK and some other countries is that there has been a rise of managerialism, diminishing the role and autonomy of the professional. In the drive to be accountable and equitable, managers are trying to prescribe and control practice in more and more detail, reducing the scope for individual reasoning. Unfortunately, this leads to general policies that, enacted as exact rules, are clumsy and insensitive at the individual case level. Again, to quote Stevenson:

> The central dilemma for child welfare workers ... is that the circumstances and needs of children are infinitely varied and unique, so that generalised policies are never a substitute for individualistic judgements and decisions. (1999: 95)

The struggle between managerial and professional control of practice is a major issue in the child protection services of many countries. The more managerialism gains control, the stronger the shift towards defensive practice and general procedures and rules that are insensitive to the needs of individual families. The professional role will be increasingly reduced to that of a bureaucrat with no scope for expert appraisal and tailored responses.

TRAINING NEEDS

The analytic and intuitive dimensions of professional expertise are associated with contrasting strategies for training, both of which are represented in the standard format for training in the helping professions. The balance and the value assigned to each of these strategies will vary according to the perceived value of each method of thinking.

Formal knowledge and aids to reasoning are best taught in the classroom. Theory and research findings can be explicitly spelled out and students tested on their ability to remember them. Case material is useful as a means of demonstrating how to apply the formal knowledge to families.

Intuitive skills are built up by experience. Students' previous experience of life is a valuable asset – a factor recognised in social work training, where mature entrants have always been welcomed. If experience is a key factor in developing the specific skills of child protection work, training needs to ensure people are exposed to lots of it. Work experience is a crucial part of training in any helping profession but this necessarily limited range of experience can be augmented by practising interviewing techniques in college and through studying vignettes and using case examples on video.

Experience on its own is not enough to develop expertise. It needs to be enhanced by critical reflection and discussion of what sense the student is making of the information. Kolb (1984) describes a learning cycle as follows: concrete experience – critical reflection on experience – action – further critical reflection. Typically, this process is conducted in supervision of the student's practice. When intuition is seen as being in sharp conflict with analytic thinking, it tends to be treated as something mystical and beyond scrutiny. In fact, it can be analysed to a considerable degree and good practitioners develop the ability to articulate and reflect critically on their intuitive thought processes.

Klein (2000: 168) suggests that the usual view of experts is that they differ from a novice in that they *know more*. Training courses then concentrate on teaching more facts, rules, and procedures. Against this view, he argues that expertise is *learning how to perceive*. The expert is able to spot patterns (that are invisible to a novice) and anomalies – things that do not fit the typical picture, and have an overall picture of the situation, past, present, and future. The two essential skills are pattern matching and mental simulation. 'Pattern matching (intuition) refers to the ability of the expert to detect typicality and to notice events that did not happen and other anomalies that violate that pattern. Mental simulation covers the ability to see events that happened previously and events that are likely to happen in the future' (2000: 149).

Consider how a novice and an expert differ in their response to an initial allegation of abuse. The novice has some guidelines on what counts as abuse and what procedures should be followed. The response will be slow and methodical, responding to the features of the case that appear on the formal guidance but with little appreciation of its unique features. The expert sees the referral as fitting a type and can swiftly make judgements about plausibility, severity, and what actions are needed and how urgently.

The case example used in Chapter 2 showed an experienced social worker responding to a step-parent adoption application. Alarm bells quickly began to ring in her head because of the anomalous behaviour of the parents. In this type of referral, parents do not usually show such hostility to the child they want to adopt. Indeed, this behaviour is so much the opposite of what is expected that it is hard to fit it into any plausible story that makes sense of the adoption request. A novice has difficulty in knowing what is or is not important or usual, except in relation to official rules.

THE WORK ENVIRONMENT

Training, at best, produces professionals at a beginner level of competence. To develop further from novice to expert needs the right work culture and organisation. Typically, further opportunities for formal training will be available from time to time. But the greatest source of learning comes from practice experience. Klein (2000: 104) lists the ways that experts learn from experience:

TABLE 9.1 **Culture of thoughtfulness scale**

Please circle the numbers in the columns that best describe your responses.

SD = Strongly disagree   **D** = Disagree   **N** = Neither   **A** = Agree   **SA** = Strongly agree

No.	Statements Describing Actions in Your Work Environment	SD	D	N	A	SA
1	The purposes of discussions are clearly described.	1	2	3	4	5
2	Alternative views on issues are sought.	1	2	3	4	5
3	Alternative views are considered carefully.	1	2	3	4	5
4	Evidence against as well as for favored views is sought.	1	2	3	4	5
5	Key terms are clearly defined.	1	2	3	4	5
6	Behaviors of interest are clearly described, with specific examples given.	1	2	3	4	5
7	Questions are clearly stated.	1	2	3	4	5
8	People identify assumptions underlying their beliefs.	1	2	3	4	5
9	Implications of proposed options are clearly described.	1	2	3	4	5
10	Getting at the "truth" is valued over "winning" an argument.	1	2	3	4	5
11	People are never punished for introducing ideas that differ from those favored by a group.	1	2	3	4	5
12	Criticisms of an argument focus on important points and are made without sarcasm or put-downs.	1	2	3	4	5
13	When available and relevant, research data are cited in support of statements and related sources are noted; appropriate documentation is provided.	1	2	3	4	5
14	Inferences made are compatible with what is known about behavior.	1	2	3	4	5
15	Group leaders/administrators do not rely on unsupported pronouncements about what is best.	1	2	3	4	5
16	Beliefs and actions are well reasoned (based on acceptable, relevant, and sufficient evidence).	1	2	3	4	5
17	The buddy-buddy system (agreement based on friendship rather than the cogency of a view) is discouraged.	1	2	3	4	5
18	Participants do not interrupt each other.	1	2	3	4	5
19	People take responsibility for describing the reasons for their beliefs/actions.	1	2	3	4	5
20	People change their mind when there is good reason to do so.	1	2	3	4	5
21	Participants thank others who point out errors in their thinking.	1	2	3	4	5
22	Reliance on questionable criteria is avoided (e.g., unfounded authority, tradition, anecdotal experience).*	1	2	3	4	5
23	Diversionary tactics are avoided (e.g., red herring, angering an opponent).*	1	2	3	4	5
24	Evasive tactics are avoided (e.g., changing the topic).*	1	2	3	4	5

FOLLOW-UP QUESTIONS

1   Which three items (highest scores) are your workplace's greatest strengths?

      a ....

      ....

      b ....

      ....

TABLE 9.1 **Continued**

    c ....

    ....

k2   Which three items (lowest scores) are your workplace's greatest weaknesses?

    a ....

    ....

    b ....

    ....

    c ....

    ....

* You could use Cells 22–24 to determine the rate per minute of informal fallacies during a discussion.

Reproduced from L. Gibbs and E. Gambrill (1999), *Critical Thinking for Social Workers*, Thousand Oaks, CA: Pine Forge Press.

- They engage in deliberate practice, so that each opportunity for practice has a goal and evaluation criteria.
- They compile an extensive experience bank.
- They obtain feedback that is accurate, diagnostic, and reasonably timely.
- They enrich their experiences by reviewing prior experiences to derive new insights and lessons from mistakes.

All of these strategies would generally be deemed aspects of good child protection practice but the extent to which they are implemented is variable and will be crucially affected by the extent to which the work environment encourages and supports them. Reflection and thinking take time, time to go over their experience, critically reviewing how they dealt with a case. What opportunities were missed? What signals were not picked up at the time? Which assessments or decisions now look questionable? Heavy caseloads and pressure to deal with cases quickly discourage this reflection. Obtaining feedback takes not only time but also co-operation from others, most noticeably a skilled supervisor. Again, the realities of many professionals' working lives make this hard to obtain. Yet without it, it is very difficult for professionals to learn from their mistakes and improve their skills.

The pervasive and fundamental aspect of all the ways people learn from experience is an open-minded attitude. Professionals need to believe that they can make mistakes and that they can improve their reasoning before they will see the value in using any of the strategies to do so. Many, if not most, will start their working lives with good intentions but whether they hold on to them will depend on the culture they find themselves working in. The increasingly common management style that sees the main function of supervision as being to check that procedures have been correctly followed, with a punitive approach to errors, undervalues the role of expertise and is totally hostile to open-minded thinking.

Gibbs and Gambrill (1999: 221) provide a 'culture of thoughtfulness scale' (Table 9.1) that lists the features of a work environment that encourage or discourage good thinking skills. It identifies aspects such as openness to alternative views, whether getting at the truth is valued more than winning an argument, and whether reference to empirical research is valued. Completing this rating scale is a useful exercise in helping agencies and individuals identify the culture around them and considering how it can be changed towards encouraging thoughtfulness.

CONCLUSION

Poor thinking tends to be characterised by a blinkered approach, considering few options, reaching conclusions too hastily, and then not paying attention to information that tells against that conclusion. Thinking can display these weaknesses whether it falls toward the analytic or the intuitive end of the continuum. Good thinking, in contrast, takes more time and effort. Thinkers must take a much more active role in searching for a wider range of evidence about the child's health and safety, in considering different assessments of the quality of parenting, and in trying to check their judgements.

Child protection workers should be like detectives, not barristers. They need to make a thorough search for the truth, with an open mind that considers different possibilities, and to test the conclusions they reach. Barristers, in contrast, are paid to defend one particular point of view, and use only the information that helps them do this. From the common criticisms from parents caught up in the child protection system, many professionals are acting more like barristers. Parents complain that they feel they are dealing with fixed minds, that the professionals seem determined to interpret everything to suit their current opinion and to ignore or discount anything the parents say that challenges it. This experience is not just frustrating for parents but also damaging to the child protection agency, whose aims are to minimise harm to children while maximising their welfare.

Another aspect of good thinking is that it helps people to be clearer about their reasoning processes, whether analytic or intuitive. Some errors are due to poor practice and should be criticised, but many are an unavoidable feature of working in an area where knowledge is so limited. If a tragedy occurs, the professional who can explain the thinking behind the decisions is better placed to defend them and to show that, although hindsight shows they were wrong, they were reasonable at the time.

An advantage of greater explicitness is that it helps to tackle discrimination and racism; again, the more open the reasoning, the easier it is to challenge and point to discriminatory assumptions. Racism and prejudices generally are conveyed more easily through intuitive judgements. Few in the child protection field are consciously racist or discriminatory but their background knowledge and assumptions are inevitably pervaded by the beliefs and attitudes of their culture and this, particularly in old imperial powers like Britain, includes many racist views.

Greater clarity about professional reasoning also helps to increase the empowerment of parents and children; this requires clearer reasoning that (a) can be explained to them and (b) they can participate in. The more intuitive and implicit the professional's thinking, the less understandable it is to users. Even if professionals decide that they have to override the wishes of children or parents, they will be better able to explain to them why their views have not been acted on.

Good thinking, I have argued, involves the full range of our intellectual skills. The theme of this book has been that both intuition and analysis are needed but that practice can be improved by shifting along the continuum towards a more analytic approach at certain points. Intuitive skills should be respected as an essential part of practice but they are not inscrutable. The more open-minded and critical the approach, the more accessible and reliable intuitive knowledge can become, thus increasing the effectiveness of the child protection system.

references

Adcock M. (1995) *Framework for Risk Assessment*. London: Wilson and James.

Aldridge M. and Wood J. (1998) *Interviewing Children: A Guide for Child Care and Forensic Practitioners*. Chichester: Wiley.

American Humane Association (1993) *Evaluation of the Pennsylvanian Approach to Risk Assessment: An Executive Summary of the Results for Project Objectives 1, 2, and 4*. Unpublished manuscript.

Aries P. (1962) *Centuries of Childhood*. London: Jonathan Cape.

Atherton C. and Klemmack D. (1982) *Research Methods in Social Work*. Lexington, MA: D.C. Heath.

Audit Commission (1994) *Seen But Not Heard: Co-ordinating Community Child Health and Social Services for Children in Need*. London: HMSO.

Bacon F. (1960 [1620]) *Novum Organum*. New York: Liberal Arts Press.

Barn R. (1990) 'Black children in local authority care: admission patterns', *New Community*, 16: 229–46.

Beard (1990):

Baron J. (1994) *Thinking and Deciding*. 2nd edn. Cambridge: Cambridge University Press.

Bayes T. (1763) 'An essay towards solving a problem in the doctrine of chances', *Philosophical Transactions of the Royal Society*, 53: 370–418 (reprinted in *Biometrica*, 1958, 45: 293–315).

Beach L. R. (1997) *The Psychology of Decision Making*. London: Sage.

Beard M. (1990) Review of Tate, *Times Literary Supplement*, 14 September, p. 968.

Beck U. (1992) *Risk Society: Towards a New Modernity*. London: Sage.

Bell M. (1999) *Child Protection, Families, and the Conference Process*. Aldershot: Ashgate.

Benoit D., Zeneah C. and Barton M. (1989) 'Maternal attachment disturbances in failure to thrive', *Infant Mental Health Journal*, 10: 185–202.

Berliner L. and Conte J. (1990) 'The process of victimization: the victim's perspective', *Child Abuse and Neglect*, 14: 29–40.

Besharov D. (1990) *Recognising Child Abuse: A Guide for the Concerned*. New York: The Free Press.

Beveridge W. (1942) *Social Insurance and Allied Services: A Report*. London: HMSO.

Birchall E. and Hallett C. (1995) *Working Together in Child Protection*. London: HMSO.

Bonoli G., George V. and Taylor-Gooby P. (2000) *European Welfare Futures*. Cambridge: Polity Press.

Booth C. (1889) *Life and Labour of the People of London*. Vol. 1. London: Macmillan.

Bowlby J. (1953) *Child Care and the Growth of Love*. London: Pelican Books.

Bowlby J. (1984) *Attachment and Loss*. 2nd edn. London: Penguin Books.

Bradbury B. and Jantti M. (1999) *Child Poverty Across Industrialised Nations*. Innocenti Occasional Papers, EPS 1971. Florence: UNICEF.

Bradbury B. and Jantti M. (2001) 'Child poverty across the industrialised world: evidence from the Luxembourg Income Study', in K. Vleminckx and T. Smeeding (eds.), *Child Well-Being, Child Poverty and Child Policy in Modern Nations*. Bristol: Policy Press.

Bridge Child Care Consultancy (1995) *Paul: Death Through Neglect*. London: Bridge Child Care Consultancy.

Briere J., Berliner L., Bulkley J., Jenny C. and Reid T. (eds.) (1996) *The APSAC Handbook on Child Maltreatment*. Thousand Oaks, CA: Sage.

Briggs C. and Cutright P. (1994) 'Structural and cultural determinants of child homicide: a cross-national analysis', *Violence and Victims*, 9: 3–16.

Browne K. and Saqi S. (1988) 'Approaches to screening for child abuse and neglect', in K. Browne, C. Davies and P. Stratton (eds.), *Early Prediction and Prevention of Child Abuse*. Chichester: Wiley.

Burns R. (200) *Introduction to Research Methods*. London: Sage.

Cabinet Office (2000) *Adoption; Prime Minister's Review*. London: Cabinet Office.

Campbell D. and Stanley J. (1966) *Experimental and Quasi-Experimental Designs for Research*. New York: Houghton Mifflin.

Cannon-Bowers J. and Salas E. (eds.) (2000) *Making Decisions under Stress; Implications for Individual and Team Training*. Washington, DC: American Psychological Association.

Carnap R. (1975) 'Testability and meaning', In H. Feigh and M. Brodbeck (eds.), *Readings in the Philosophy of Science*. New York: Appleton-Century-Crofts.

Casscells W., Schoenberger A. and Grayboys T. (1978) 'Interpretation by physicians of clinical laboratory results', *New England Journal of Medicine*, 299: 999–1000.

Chalmers A. (1983) *What Is This Thing Called Science?* Milton Keynes: Open University Press.

Chand A. (2000) 'The over representation of Black children in the child protection system; possible causes, consequences and solutions', *Child and Family Social Work*, 5: 67–78.

Charities Organisation Society (1890) *Form no. 28, Notice to Persons Applying for Assistance*. In *COS Forms, Papers, Investigating Tickets, Byelaws Almanak etc. 1877–90* in the possession of the Family Welfare Association (formerly COS) Denison House, London.

Cleaver H. and Freeman P. (1995) *Parental Perspectives in Cases of Suspected Child Abuse*. London: HMSO.

Corby B. (1987) *Working with Child Abuse*. Milton Keynes: Open University Press.

Daly M. and Wilson M. (1985) 'Child abuse and other risks of not living with both parents', *Ethnology and Sociobiology*, 6: 197–210.

Dawes R. (1988) *Rational Choice in an Uncertain World*. Orlando, FL: Harcourt Brace Jovanovich.

Deacon B. with Hulse M. and Stubbs P. (1997) *Global Social Policy*. London: Sage.

Department of Health (1988) *Report of the Inquiry into Child Abuse in Cleveland, 1987*. London: HMSO.

Department of Health (1995) *Child Protection: Messages from Research*. London: HMSO.

Department of Health (1999) *Working Together to Safeguard Children: A Guide for Inter-Agency Working to Safeguard and Promote the Welfare of Children*. London: Department of Health.

Department of Health (2000a) *Assessing Children in Need and their Families: Practice Guidance*. London: HMSO.

Department of Health (2000b) *Framework for the Assessment of Children in Need and their Families*. London: HMSO.

Department of Health (2001) *Studies Informing the Framework for the Assessment of Children in Need and their Families*. London: HMSO.

Department of Health and Social Security (1974) *Report of the Committee of Inquiry into the Care and Supervision Provided in Relation to Maria Colwell*. London: HMSO.

Department of Health and Social Security (1975) *Report of the Committee of Inquiry into the Provision and Co-ordination of Services to the Family of John George Aukland*. London: HMSO.

Department of Health and Social Security (1979) *The Report of the Committee of Inquiry into the Actions of the Authorities and Agencies Relating to Darryn James Clarke*. London: HMSO, Cmnd 7730.

Department of Health and Social Security (1985) *Social Work Decisions in Child Care: Recent Research Findings and the Implications*. London: HMSO.

Department of Health and Social Security (1988) *Working Together: A Guide to Inter-Agency Co-operation for the Protection of Children*. London: HMSO.

Department of Social Security (1999) *Opportunity for All: Tackling Poverty and Social Exclusion*. London: HMSO.

Dingwall R., Eekelaar J. and Murray T. (1983) *The Protection of Children: State Intervention and Family Life*. Oxford: Blackwell.

Dreyfus H. and Dreyfus S. (1986) *Mind over Machine: The Power of Human Intuition and Expertise in the Era of the Computer*. New York: The Free Press.

Egeland B. and Sroufe L. (1981) 'Attachment and early maltreatment', *Child Development,* 52: 44–52.

Egeland B. and Sroufe L. (1983) 'Developmental consequences of differential patterns of maltreatment', *Child Abuse and Neglect,* 7: 459–469.

Erikson M., Egeland B. and Pianta R. (1989) 'The effects of maltreatment on the development of young children', In D. Cichetti, and V. Carlson (eds.), *Child Maltreatment: Theory and Research on the Causes and Consequences of Child Abuse and Neglect.* New York: Cambridge University Press.

Esping-Anderson G. (1990) *The Three Worlds of Welfare: Capitalism.* Cambridge: Polity Press.

European Union Commission (1993) *Growth, Competitiveness, and Employment.* Brussels: European Union.

Eysenck H. (1986) *Decline and Fall of the Freudian Empire.* London: Pelican Books.

Farmer E. and Owen M. (1995) *Child Protection Practice: Private Risks and Public Remedies – Decision Making, Intervention and Outcome in Child Protection Work.* London: HMSO.

Farrell B. (1981) *The Standing of Psychoanalysis.* Oxford: Oxford University Press.

Field F. (1989) *The Emergence of Britain's Underclass.* Oxford: Blackwell.

Finkelhor S. (1994) 'The international epidemiology of child sexual abuse', *Child Abuse and Neglect,* 18: 837–41.

Fischer J. (1973) 'Is casework effective? a review', *Social Work,* 1: 5–20.

Fischoff B. (1996) 'The real world: what good is it?', *Organizational Behaviour and Human Decision Processes,* 65: 232–48.

Fluke J. et al. (1993) 'Evaluation of the Pennsylvania approach to risk assessment', in T. Tatara (ed.), *Seventh National Roundtable on Child Protective Services Risk Assessment: Summary of Highlights.* Washington, DC: American Public Welfare Association. pp. 113–72.

Fukuyama F. (1992) *The End of History and the Last Man.* New York: Free Press.

Furnis T. (1991) *The Multi-Professional Handbook of Child Sexual Abuse.* London: Routledge.

Gabarino J., Guttman E. and Seely J. (1986) *The Psychologically Battered Child.* San Francisco, CA: Jossey-Bass.

Gabarino J. (ed.) (1992) *Children and Families in the Social Environment.* 2nd edn. New York: Aldine de Gruyter.

Gambrill E. (1990) *Critical Thinking in Clinical Practice.* San Francisco, CA: Jossey-Bass.

Gelles R. (1975) 'The social construction of child abuse', *American Journal of Orthopsychiatry,* 45: 363–71.

Geyer R., Ingerbritsen C. and Moses J. (1999) *Globalization, Europeanization and the End of Scandinavian Social Democracy?* Basingstoke: Macmillan.

Gibbons J., Conroy S. and Bell C. (1995a) *Operating the Child Protection System: A Study of Child Protection Practices in English Local Authorities.* London: HMSO.

Gibbons J., Gallagher B., Bell C. and Gordon D. (1995b) *Development after Physical Abuse in Early Childhood.* London: HMSO.

Gibbs L. and Gambrill E. (1999) *Critical Thinking for Social Workers, Exercises for the Helping Profession.* Thousand Oaks, CA: Pine Forge Publications.

Giddens A. (1990) *The Consequences of Modernity.* Cambridge: Polity Press.

Giddens A. (1999) *Runaway World: How Globalisation Is Reshaping Our Lives.* London: Profile.

Giddens A. (ed.) (2001) *The Global Third Way Debate.* Cambridge: Polity Press.

Gigerenzer G., Todd P. and the ABC Research Group (1999) *Simple Heuristics That Make Us Smart.* Oxford: Oxford University Press.

Goddard C., Saunders B., Stanley J. and Tucci J. (1999) 'Structured risk assessment procedures: instruments of abuse?', *Child Abuse Review,* 8: 251–63.

Goldstein H. (1986) 'Towards the integration of theory and practice: a humanistic approach', *Social Work,* 14: 352–7.

Gough I. (1998) 'Social policy and economic policy', in Alcock P., Erskine A. and Mays M. (eds), *The Student's Compendium to Social Policy.* Oxford: Blackwell. pp. 107–14.

Gough R. (1993) *Child Abuse Interventions.* Edinburgh, HMSO.

Greenland C. (1987) *Preventing CAN Deaths: An International Study of Deaths Due to Child Abuse and Neglect.* London: Tavistock.

Grove W. and Meehl P. (1996) 'Comparative efficiency of informal (subjective, impressionistic) and formal (mechanical, algorithmic) prediction procedures', *Psychology, Public Policy and Law*, 2: 293–323.

Grunbaum A. (1985) *The Foundations of Psychoanalysis*. Berkeley, MA: University of California Press.

Hacking I. (1999) *The Social Construction of What?* Cambridge, CA: Harvard University Press.

Hagall A. (1998) *Dangerous Care: Reviewing the Risks to Children from Their Carers*. London: The Bridge Child Care Development Service.

Hallett C. (1995) *Interagency Co-ordination in Child Protection*. London: HMSO.

Hammond K. (1996) *Human Judgement and Social Policy: Irreducible Uncertainty, Inevitable Error, Unavoidable Injustice*. Oxford: Oxford University Press.

Hammond J., Keeney R. and Raiffa H. (1999) *Smart Choices: A Practical Guide to Making Better Decisions*. Boston, MA: Harvard Business School Press.

Hastie R. (2001) 'Problems for judgement and decision making', *Annual Review of Psychology*, 52: 653–83.

Hetherington R., Cooper A., Smith P. and Wilford G. (1997) *Protecting Children: Messages from Europe*. Lyme Regis, Dorset: Russell House Publishing.

Hill M. (1990) 'The manifest and latent lessons of child abuse inquiries', *British Journal of Social Work*, 20: 197–213.

Hirst P. and Thompson G. (1999) *Globalization in Question*. Cambridge: Polity Press.

Hogarth R. (1981) 'Beyond discrete biases: functional and dysfunctional aspects of judgmental heuristics', *Psychological Bulletin*, 90: 197–217.

Holway J. (1963) *Sermons on Several Occasions by Rev. John Wesley: Modern Translation*. London: Methodist Press.

Home Office (1945) *Report by Sir William Monckton on the Circumstances Which Led to the Boarding Out of Dennis and Terence O'Neill at Bank Farm, Masterlely and the Steps Taken to Supervise Their Welfare*. London: HMSO.

Howe D. (1987) *An Introduction to Social Work Theory*. Aldershot: Wildwood House.

Howson C. and Urbach P. (1989) *Scientific Reasoning: The Bayesian Approach*. La Salle, IL: Open Court.

ISPCAN (1994) *Child Abuse and Neglect*. New York: Pergamon.

Iwaniec D. (1983) 'Social and psychological factors in the aetiology and management of children who fail to thrive'. Unpublished PhD thesis, University of Leicester.

Iwaniec D. (1995) *The Emotionally Abused and Neglected Child: Identification, Assessment and Intervention*. Chichester: John Wiley.

Janis I. (1982) *Groupthink: Psychological Studies of Policy Decisions and Fiascoes*. Boston, MA: Houghton Mifflin.

Janis I. and Mann L. (1977) *Decision Making, A Psychological Analysis of Conflict, Choice, and Commitment*. New York: The Free Press.

Johnson H. and Chisholm P. (1989) 'Family homicide statistics, Canada', *Canadian Social Trends*, Autumn: 17–18.

Johnson W. and Clancy T. (1988) *A Study To Find Improved Methods of Screening and Disposing of Reports of Child Maltreatment in the Emergency Program in Alameda County, California*. Oakland, CA: Alameda County Social Services.

Johnson W. (1996) 'Risk assessment research: progress and future directions', *Protecting Children*, 12: 14–19.

Jones A. (1945) *Juvenile Delinquency and the Law*. London: Penguin.

Jones E., Rock L., Shaver K., Goethals G. and Ward L. (1968) 'Pattern of performance and ability attribution: an unexpected primacy effect', *Journal of Personality and Social Psychology*, 6: 107–18.

Kahneman D., Slonic P. and Tversky A. (1990) *Judgement under Uncertainty: Heuristics and Biases*. Cambridge: Cambridge University Press.

Kamerman S. (1996) 'Child and family policies: an international overview', in E. Zigler, S. Kagan and N. Hall (eds.) *Children, Families, and Government; Preparing for the Twenty-First Century*. Cambridge: Cambridge University Press.

Keller R., Cicchenelli L. and Gardner D. (1988) *A Comparative Analysis of Risk Assessment Models: Phase 1 Report*. Denver, CO: Applied Research Associates.

Keller L. and Ho J. (1988) 'Decision problem structuring: generating options', *Systems, Man and Cybernetics*, 18: 715–28.

Kempe C., Silverman F., Steel B., Droegmueller W. and Silver H. (1962) 'The battered child syndrome', *Journal of the American Medical Association*, 181: 17–24.

Kempson E. (1996) *Life on a Low Income*. York: Joseph Rowntree Foundation.

Kiernan K. (1996) 'Family change: parenthood, partnership and policy', in D. Halpern et al. (eds.), *Options for Britain: A Strategic Policy Review*. Dartmouth: Dartmouth Press.

Klein G. (2000) *Sources of Power: How People Make Decisions*. Cambridge, MA: MIT Press.

Klein M. and Stern L. (1971) 'Low birth weight and the battered child syndrome', *American Journal for Diseases of Children*, 122: 15–18.

Kluger M., Alexander G. and Curtis P. (eds.) (2001) *What Works in Child Welfare*. Washington, DC: Child Welfare League of America.

Kolb D. (1984) *Experiential Learning: Experience as the Source of Learning and Development*. Englewood Cliffs, NJ: Prentice-Hall.

Koriat A., Lichenstein S. and Fischoff B. (1980) 'Reasons for confidence', *Journal of Experimental Psychology: Human Learning and Memory*, 6: 107–118.

Korbin J. (1991) 'Cross-cultural perspectives and research directions for the 21st century', *Child Abuse and Neglect*, 15, Suppl. 1: 67–77.

Krimmerman L. (ed.) (1975) *The Nature and Scope of Social Science: A Critical Anthology*. New York: Appleton-Century-Crofts.

Kuhn T. (1978) *The Essential Tension*. Chicago: University of Chicago Press.

Lewis A. (1994) *Chairing Child Protection Conferences*. Aldershot: Avebury.

Local Government Association (1997) *Removing the Barriers: The Case for a New Deal for Social Services and Social Security*. London: Local Government Association.

London Borough of Brent (1985) *A Child in Trust: The Report of the Panel of Inquiry into the Circumstances Surrounding the Death of Jasmine Beckford*. London: London Borough of Brent.

London Borough of Greenwich (1987) *A Child in Mind: The Report of the Commission of Inquiry into the Circumstances Surrounding the Death of Kimberley Carlile*. London: London Borough of Greenwich.

London Borough of Lambeth (1987) *Whose Child? The Report of the Public Inquiry into the Death of Tyra Henry*. London: London Borough of Lambeth.

Lyons P., Doueck H. and Wodarski J. (1996) 'Risk assessment for child protective services: a review of the empirical literature on instrument performance', *Social Work Research*, 20: 143–55.

Macdonald G. (2001) *Effective Interventions for Child Abuse and Neglect*. Chichester: Wiley.

Marsh P. and Triseliotis J. (1996) *Ready to Practise? Social Workers and Probation Officers: Their Training and First Year in Work*. Aldershot: Avebury.

Maslach C., Schaufeli W. and Leiter M. (2001) 'Job burnout', *Annual Review of Psychology*, 52: 397–422.

McDonald T. and Marks J. (1991) 'A review of risk factors assessed in child protective services', *Social Services Review*, 65: 112–32.

Meadows R. (1997) *The ABC of Child Abuse*. London: British Medical Association.

Meehl P. (1986) 'Causes and effects of my disturbing little book', *Journal of Personality Assessment*, 50: 370–5.

Meehl P. (1992) 'Cliometric metatheory: the actuarial approach to empirical, history-based philosophy of science', *Psychological Reports*, 71: 339–467.

Meehl P. (1997) 'Credentialed persons, credentialed knowledge', *Clinical Psychology: Science and Practice*, 4: 91–8.

Middleton L., Ashworth K. and Braithwaite I. (1997) *Small Fortunes: Spending on Children, Childhood, Poverty and Parental Sacrifice*. York: Joseph Rowntree Foundation.

Milne R. and Bull R. (1999) *Investigative Interviewing: Psychology and Practice*. Chichester: Wiley.

Minty B. and Pattinson G. (1994) 'The nature of child neglect', *British Journal of Social Work*, 24: 733–47.

Modood T. and Berthoud R. (eds.) (1997) *Diversity and Disadvantage; Ethnic Minorities in Britain.* London: Policy Studies Institute.

Monteleone J. and Brodeur A. (1998) *Child Maltreatment; A Clinical Guide and Reference.* St. Louis, MO: G.W. Medical Publishing Inc.

Morgan M. (1995) *How To Interview Sexual Abuse Victims.* Thousand Oaks, CA: Sage.

Morrison T. (1990) 'The emotional effects of child protection work on the workers', *Practice,* 4: 253–71.

Moscovici S. and Zavalloni M. (1969) 'The group as polarizer of attitudes', *Journal of Personality and Social Psychology,* 12: 125–35.

Munro E. (1996) 'Avoidable and unavoidable mistakes in child protection work', *British Journal of Social Work,* 26: 795–810.

Munro E. (1998) *Understanding Social Work: An Empirical Approach.* London: Continuum Press.

Munro E. (1999) 'Common errors of reasoning in child protection work', *Child Abuse and Neglect,* 23 (8): 745–58.

Murray C. (1990) *The Emerging British Underclass.* London: IEA, Health and Welfare Unit.

Murray Parkes C. (1986) *Bereavement: Studies of Grief in Adult Life.* London: Penguin Books.

Myers J. (ed.) (1994) *The Backlash: Child Protection under Fire.* London: Sage.

National Commission of Inquiry into the Prevention of Child Abuse (1996) *Childhood Matters, Vol. 1.* London: HMSO.

National Research Council (1993) *Understanding Child Abuse and Neglect.* Washington, DC: National Academy Press.

Navarro V. (2000) 'Neoliberalism, "globalization", unemployment, inequalities, and the welfare state', *International Journal of Health Services,* 28 (4): 607–82.

Newell A. and Simon H. (1972) *Human Problem Solving.* Englewood Cliffs, NJ: Prentice-Hall.

Newton-Smith W. (1981) *The Rationality of Science.* London: Routledge and Kegan Paul.

Nisbett R. and Ross L. (1980) *Human Inference: Strategies and Shortcomings of Human Judgement.* Englewood Cliffs, NJ: Prentice-Hall.

Nottinghamshire Area Child Protection Committee (1994) *Report of Overview Group into the Circumstances Surrounding the Death of Leanne White.* Nottingham: Nottinghamshire Country Council.

OECD (1999) *Economic Survey: Sweden.* Paris: Organisation for Economic Co-operation and Development.

Parsloe P. (ed.) (1999) *Risk Assessment in Social Care and Social Work.* London: Jessica Kingsley Publishers.

Parton N. (1985) *The Politics of Child Abuse.* London: Macmillan.

Parton N. (1991) *Governing the Family: Child Care, Child Protection and the State.* London: Macmillan.

Parton N. (ed.) (1997) *Child Protection and Family Support.* London: Routledge.

Parton N., Thorpe D. and Wattam C. (1997) *Child Protection: Risk and the Moral Order.* London: Macmillan.

Piachaud D. and Sutherland H. (2000) *How Effective Is the British Government's Attempt to Reduce Child Poverty.* Case Paper 38. London: London School of Economics.

Plous S. (1983) *The Psychology of Judgement and Decision Making.* New York: McGraw-Hill.

Polanyi M. (1967) *The Tacit Dimension.* Garden City, NY: Doubleday.

Popper K. (1963) *Conjectures and Refutations.* London: Routledge and Kegan Paul.

Pringle K. (1998) *Children and Social Welfare in Europe.* Buckingham: Open University Press.

Putnam H. (1978) *Meaning and the Moral Sciences.* London: Routledge and Kegan Paul.

Rhodes M. (1996) 'Globalization and West European welfare states: a critical review of recent debates', *Journal of European Social Policy,* 6 (4): 305–27.

Richmond M. (1917) *Social Diagnosis.* New York: Russell Sage Foundation.

Rose S. and Meezan W. (1996) 'Variations in perceptions of child neglect', *Child Welfare,* 75: 139–60.

Rosen H. (1981) 'How social workers use cues to determine child abuse', *Social Work Research and Abstracts,* 17: 4.

Rosenberg A. (1988) *Philosophy of Social Science.* Cambridge: Clarendon Press.

Rowntree S. (1902) *Poverty: A Study of Town Life*. London: Macmillan.

Rumgay J. and Munro E. (2001) 'The lion's den: professional defences in the treatment of dangerous patients', *Journal of Forensic Psychiatry*, 12: 357–78.

Rushton A. and Nathan J. (1996) 'The supervision of child protection work', *British Journal of Social Work*, 26: 357–74.

Schaffer H.R. (1998) *Making Decisions about Children*. Oxford: Blackwell.

Schaufeli W. and Enzmann D. (1998) *The Burnout Companion to Study and Practice: A Critical Analysis*. Philadelphia: Taylor and Francis.

Scottish Office (1992) *The Report of the Inquiry into the Removal of Children from Orkney in February 1991*. Edinburgh: HMSO.

Seabrook J. (2001) *Children of Other Worlds: Exploitation in the Global Market*. London: Pluto Press.

Secker J. (1993) *From Theory to Practice in Social Work*. Aldershot: Avebury.

Simon H. (1957) *Models of Man: Social and Rational*. New York: Wiley.

Simon H. (1990) 'Invariants of human behaviour', *Annual Review of Psychology*, 41: 1–19.

Sobell L. (1996) 'Bridging the gap between scientists and practitioners: the challenge before us'. *Behaviour Therapy*, 27: 297–320.

Social Services Inspectorate (1993) *Evaluating Child Protection Services: Findings and Issues*. London: Department of Health.

Steinhauer P., Leitenberger M., Manglicas E., Pauker J., Smith R. and Boncalves L. (1993) *Guidelines for Assessing Parenting Capacity*. Toronto: Toronto Parenting Capacity Assessment Project.

Stevenson O. (1998) *Neglected Children: Issues and Dilemmas*. Oxford: Blackwell.

Stevenson O. (ed.) (1999) *Child Welfare in the UK*. Oxford: Blackwell Science.

Stiemerling M. (2000) *Globalisation, Social Policy, and the Power of Ideology*. London: London School of Economics, MSc dissertation.

Sutherland S. (1992) *Irrationality: The Enemy Within*. London: Constable.

Taylor H. and Russell J. (1939) 'The relationship of validity coefficients to the practical applications of tests of selection', *Journal of Applied Psychology*, 23: 565–78.

Temrin H., Buchmayer S. and Enquist M. (2000) 'Step-parents and infanticide: new data contradict evolutionary predictions', *Proceedings of the Royal Society London*, 267: 943–5.

Thoburn J. (1990) *Success and Failure in Permanent Family Placement*. Aldershot: Avebury.

Thorpe D. (1994) *Evaluating Child Protection*. Milton Keynes: Open University Press.

Thorpe D. and Bilson A. (1998) 'From protection to concern: child protection careers without apologies', *Children and Society*, 12: 373–86.

Titmuss R. (1958) *Essays on the Welfare State*. London: Allen and Unwin.

United Nations (1989) *The United Nations Convention on the Rights of the Child*. New York: United Nations.

UNICEF (1992) *The State of the World's Children*. Oxford: Oxford University Press.

UNICEF (1997) *Children at Risk in Central and Eastern Europe: Perils and Promises*. Florence, Italy: UNICEF.

Vleminckx K. and Smeeding T. (eds.) (2001) *Child Well-Being, Child Poverty and Child Policy in Modern Nations*. Bristol: Policy Press.

Waldfogel J. (1998) *The Future of Child Protection*. Cambridge, MA: Harvard University Press.

Walker J., McCarthy P., Morgan W. and Timms N. (1995) *In Pursuit of Quality: Improving Practice Teaching in Social Work*. London: CCETSW.

Wandsworth Area Child Protection Committee (1990) *The Report of the Stephanie Fox Practice Review*. London: London Borough of Wandsworth.

Wattam C. and Thorpe D. (1996) *Making and Receiving Child Protection Referrals*. Lancaster: Lancaster University Publications.

Wells S. (1988) 'Factors influencing the response of child protective service workers to reports of abuse and neglect', in G. Hotaling et al.. *Coping with Family Violence: Research and Policy Perspectives*. Thousand Oaks, CA: Sage.

Wells S., Stein T., Fluke J. and Downing J. (1989) 'Screening in child protective services', *Social Work*, 34: 45–48.

Wells S. and Anderson T. (1992) *Model Building in Child Protective Services Intake and Investigation. Final Report to the National Center on Child Abuse and Neglect for Grant #90–CA-1407.* Washington, DC: American Bar Association Centre on Children and the Law.

Wilensky H. (1975) *The Welfare State and Equality: Structural and Ideological Roots of Public Expenditure.* Berkeley, CA: University of California Press.

Woods D., Johannesen L., Cook R. and Sarter N. (1993) *Behind Human Error: Cognitive Systems, Computers and Hindsight.* State-of-the-Art Report. Dayton, OH: CSERIAC.

Zigler E., Kagan S. and Hall N. (eds.) (1996) *Children, Families, and Government: Preparing for the Twenty-First Century.* Cambridge: Cambridge University Press.

Zuravin S., Orme J. and Hegar R. (1995) 'Disposition of child physical abuse reports: review of the literature and test of a predictive model', *Children and Youth Services Review*, 17: 547–66.

Zurriff G. (1990) *Behaviourism: A Conceptual Reconstruction.* New York: Columbia University Press.

index